Constitutional Issues in Federal Management of Domestic Terrorism Incidents

Constitutional Issues in Federal Management of Domestic Terrorism Incidents

James F. McDonnell

iUniverse, Inc.
New York Lincoln Shanghai

Constitutional Issues in Federal Management of Domestic Terrorism Incidents

iUniverse, Inc.

For information address:
iUniverse, Inc.
2021 Pine Lake Road, Suite 100
Lincoln, NE 68512
www.iuniverse.com

ISBN: 0-595-31628-X

FOR DEIRDRE

Contents

Introduction

This book was written as a thesis for a master's degree, it was started in June of 2001 and finished in April of 2002. The original intent of this work was to cause a discussion about the lack of a comprehensive policy and corresponding laws for preventing and responding to domestic terrorism. The work was outlined prior to the devastating terrorist attacks of September 11, 2001 and was completed prior to the announcement by President Bush that a Department of Homeland Security was to be created.

At the start of writing this book I was the Director of National Security Programs for a non-profit university consortium and I am the currently Director of the Protective Security Division at the Department of Homeland Security. This writing represents my personal views before and immediately after the attacks and as such do not take into account the changes that the government has undertaken. The book remains as it was written without any changes to reflect the new laws and policies since the creation of the Department.

This is not a critique of any individuals; it is an analysis of the policy that had developed for the management of terrorist incidents. I had thought for a time that I would not publish this work but as time goes on I believe the discussion I sought to begin in 2001 is still one worthy of consideration and that writings like this will assist in the future analysis how America's leaders planned for and responded to the threat of terrorism in the homeland.

1

The American Federal System

As an introduction to a discussion of the role of the American national government in responding to terrorism, we must first trace the evolution of the American Federal System. This chapter will examine that evolution, with particular attention to those aspects that describe how our Federal System is currently prepared to deal with domestic terrorism.

In the American Constitution, the people established a system of separate governments, the national, and the States and local governments, already in existence, sharing powers vertically and horizontally. The powers of the national government were delegated to it in the Constitution. The States retained all powers not given to the national government. While State powers were not made specific, it was generally accepted that they included responsibility for the welfare and security of their citizens.

States exercise many of their powers through local governments. Some States more rural and less dense populations have strong county governments. Others with dense populations and great urban centers use municipal governments. The method of distributing power within the state and the resulting government structure reflects both cultural and economic differences between the states. Key factors that determine the best method of governing are whether the economic base is agricultural or industrial, the density of population, and ethnic and religious backgrounds.

The United States is large and diverse and the type of government we have reflects that diversity. The diversity of the United States is strength, but it is also provides challenges to operating an effective national government. A one-size-fits-all approach in the American Federal System will not work in many areas.

An examination of the role of the federal government in protecting the public must begin with an understanding of the nature of the American Federal System. How this system was conceived, what the intent was in the establishment of such a system and how has it evolved into what we see today, a massive federal system, are all issues to be addressed in the first chapter of this thesis. An analysis of the division of powers between State and Federal Government will provide the basis for discussion in the following chapters on the best method for the Federal response to terrorism within the borders of the Untied States.

During the early development of the American Federal system the states retained most governmental powers. In Alexis De Tocqueville's famous essay on the American political system he wrote, "state authority is the rule and federal government is the exception."[1] This statement reflects a general understanding of the role of the national government in the early days of the American democracy. In the creation of a federal system in America, the delegates to the Constitutional Conventions sought to establish an effective national government while preserving the prerogatives of the individual States to manage their internal affairs. Madison described the distribution of power between the Federal and State Governments in their words, "The powers delegated by the proposed Constitution to the federal government are few and defined. Those which are to remain in the state governments are numerous and indefinite."[2]

Two basic principles of the American Federal System are that power should reside as close to the people as practicable, and that no power should be absolute.

Public education serves as one example that demonstrates a division of responsibility between levels of government and is consistent with the first principle that power should reside close to the people. According to the American Schools Directory, there are approximately 108,000 public schools in the United States[3]. Using a Washington area school system as an example of how school systems are funded highlights the division of responsibilities between the various levels of government. In Fairfax County Virginia only 6.1% of the revenue for public education is federal, the rest is provided by the State or County governments[4]. The federal funds provided are not for general education and welfare. They are provided to offset the costs to Fairfax County of educating children of military and other federal employees that do not contribute to the local tax base[5] or to fund special educational programs mandated by the federal government.[6] The education of American students is a local issue, with significant assistance from the State but very little from the Federal Government. Chapter III of this thesis will discuss in detail a Supreme Court decision that weighs heavily on the argument that schools and activities that take place in schools are a governmental power reserved to the States, not the Federal Government. The Court cited the vast number of schools and the diversity of local and regional issues as primary reason that the education system and its management must be local, close to the people it affects[7]. In the area of public education the Constitution is silent, no power is delegated to the central government for the purpose of educating the citizens and the result is a locally managed, nationwide system that by most measures is extremely effective.

The second basic principle of the American Federal System is that no single office can wield too much power. Checks and balances were built into the government to prevent any branch from excesses. There are almost no functions within the American Federal System that do not require the involvement of at least two branches of government. While the President has the authority to manage the departments within the executive branch, he must submit his nominations to head agencies to the Senate and he must ask Congress to appropriate funds to be spent by the administration. The Congress must present proposed laws to the President, who may approve or veto.

The central government may expand the scope of its authorities by its own interpretation of them. For the central government to assume new powers, previously reserved to the States, an amendment to the Constitution in necessarily a process that requires the consent of the States.

While this elaborate system of checks and balances may prevent systemic abuses it does not always check incremental growth nor does it prevent short-term abuse. For example, the Framers provided the President with the authority to make appointments to offices within his administration during periods that the Senate was in recess. Given the difficultly of travel in the late eighteenth century it made sense to allow the President the latitude to make an appointment in order to keep the government functioning effectively in the Senate's absence. The Framers did not envision executive power as a way to place persons in office that could not be confirmed by the Senate through the normal process. Hamilton devotes a significant section of Federalist No. 67 to the argument that the "recess appointment" powers granted the executive are "for the purpose of establishing an auxiliary method of appointment" and "as vacancies might happen IN THEIR RECESS, which it might be said necessary for the public service to fill without delay."[8] President Clinton's use of the recess appointment on several occasions provides an example of one branch's authority encroaching on that of another,but the wisdom of the Framers ensured that even though such powers could be abused, that abuse would be limited in duration.[9]

The Framers Intent

It is clear from many of the Framers own words that their original intent was to create a hybrid government, not national and not federal.[10] The intent was a government that contained elements of both a national system and a confederacy. Madison's Federalist 39 discusses in detail the limitations on the new central government as it was conceived. In it, he describes the method of selection or appointment of members of the government as "national" in the House of Representatives who are directly elected by people they represent, and Federal in the case of the Senate, being appointed by state legislatures to represent the States. In the case of the President the electoral system provides for a hybrid of both federal and national features. The Constitution itself is federal in nature, as it is a document that required the acceptance by the States, described by Madison as "sovereigns". Madison also discusses the operation of the central government as having both federal and national attributes, being very careful to highlight the fact that the States retain certain prerogatives through the Federal system. [11]

The representatives to the Constitutional Convention were not representatives of the people, but delegations from the States. This distinction is very important in an analysis of how powers in the central government are derived. Representatives of the States met to determine what roles and powers should be vested in a central government. The question asked in the drafting of a constitution was "what are the functions that should be solely within the purview of a central government?" By asking this question one must consider the implications of the answer. The powers that needed to be delegated[12] to the central government would be limited to those that would be beyond the ability of the States to manage individually.

When discussing the Framer's intent, it is tempting to look only at the text of the Constitution and the Federalist Papers as source documents. The shortfall of using this method is that one only views the Constitution in its final form along with a series of letters seeking to gain support for that final form. What is missing in such an analysis is a review of what was intentionally left out of the document. Madison's Notes on the Convention[13] give insight to what the Framers discussed, and what they chose not to include in the way of Federal powers. This baseline analysis will be important for understanding the evolution of those powers and the claim of Framer's intent throughout that evolution.

First and foremost was the discussion of whether to retain sovereignty within the States themselves. The delegates were in general agreement that the Articles of Confederation did not provide enough authority for an effective central government.[14] There was significant discussion regarding the creation of a national government that would assume all powers of the States. A segment of the Framers took the position that the federal government was not assuming powers previously reserved to the several States because the States were never truly independent. This position was articulated by Rufus King of Massachusetts. In arguing that the central government should replace the States, he claimed that "the States were not 'Sovereigns' in the sense contended for by some. They did not possess the peculiar features of sovereignty. They could not make war, nor peace, nor alliances nor treaties." In the same debate James Wilson cited and read from the Declaration of Independence "observing, thereon that the *United Colonies* were declared to be free and independent, not *individually* but *Unitedly* and that they were confederated as they were independent." [15] While some argued that the existence of sovereign States was a fallacy, others debated the inevitable impact on the States by the creation of a central government. George Read put forth that "too much attachment is betrayed to the State Government. We must look past their continuance. A national government must soon of necessity swallow all of them up. They will soon be reduced to the mere office of electing the national Senate." This position was rebuffed by Charles Cotesworth Pinckney who "wished to have a good national Government and at the same time to leave a considerable share of power in the States."[16]

The decision to retain the States as individual entities with powers and authorities was a well-deliberated decision. The Framers decided to limit the authority that would be delegated to a central government after considering the alternatives, such as eliminating the States as independent bodies. Thus the role of the States was a key consideration in the development of the American Federal System. The Constitution does not describe the roles of the States because the document was designed to assign limited authorities to a central government. By being silent on the powers retained by the States, the Framers did not need to address a list of State authorities.

Madison did not rely on his Notes during his lifetime and only occasionally referenced the discussions that took place during the 1787 convention. One may conclude from this, as does Leonard Levy[17], that Madison thought the text more important than the discussion. Though reasonable, it cannot be construed to mean that any discussion that took place in the Convention should not be considered in understanding the Constitution. The fact that the delegates did consider and discuss the division of powers between the States and the central government must lead one to the conclusion that the resulting text, and the restrictions it imposes on the central government, was completely intentional. The delegates did not envisage an all-powerful central government, rather one that had the requisite authority to conduct the government operations within its purview, but no more.

On the question of the functions of the central government, a basic principle followed by the founders was that the powers delegated to the central would be limited to those that could not be effectively managed by the individual States. The first and most obvious area that the central government should have responsibility for was the conduct of international affairs. While the Framers seemed comfortable with the assignment of the international affairs or national security powers to the central government, they retained a level of indirect oversight by the States. All treaties negotiated and all ambassadorial assignments made by the executive would be subject to ratification of the Senate, a body envisioned as representing the interest of the individual States.[18] The net effect of the division of powers between the central government and the States concerning national security interests is that the executive was given the authorities necessary to conduct foreign policy to include waging war but the power was not absolute and not executed without the indirect approval of the States, through the Senate.

The second area of responsibility that fell to the central government was the regulation of interstate commerce. As with international affairs and the common defense, it was not feasible for the States to trade and negotiate trade treaties with other countries as individual entities. The conduct of trade between the States required laws and regulations that prohibited restrictions between the States. The Federal control of commerce has rested with the Congress without substantial changes or challenge. What has been at issue regarding the regulation of commerce has been what fits into the definition of interstate commerce.

The Supreme Court has supported the federal role in regulating commerce in numerous cases dating back to 1824. Justice Marshall defined it as "commercial intercourse between nations, and parts of nations…" and in his ruling on Gibbons[19] defined the role of the Congress in regulating commerce. The Court has followed the precedent established in Gibbons in a consistently, usually allowing the Congress broad discretion in regulating and defining what interstate commerce is. A discussion to follow on the United States v. Lopez case will outline in more detail the extent to which the Court has allowed Congress to assume greater authority under the Commerce Clause, and where it has applied some limitations.

In summarizing the original intent, it is clear that the Framers did intend for the federal government to have the authorities required to protect the security of the nation and to regulate commerce among the States and with other nations. The Framers did not intend to vest in the federal government the authorities associated with the general welfare of the citizens, including public safety.

The Changing Relationship Between the State and Federal Governments

The relationship between the State and the Federal governments has changed significantly throughout the history of the United States. This section will discuss three significant crises that each precipitated a fundamental change in the roles and relationships of the different levels of government; the Nullification Crisis of the 1830s, the Secession Crisis in 1860 and the resulting Civil War, and the Great Depression and the resultant New Deal programs.

The Nullification Crisis and Federal Law Supremacy

The nullification crisis of the 1830s was the first test of the ability of a State to ignore the laws enacted by the central government. In the years immediately following the War of 1812, Congress began to regulate international commerce through the use of tariffs. By adding a tariff, or import tax, to selected goods Congress could ensure that the goods manufactured domestically were sold at a competitive price. While this policy worried some southern legislators, it was generally accepted as necessary to allow industry to develop in the United States. Without any protection of American industry from foreign competition, factories would certainly close and all hope of long-term economic growth and independence from Europe would be lost.

Following the war of 1812, the majority of representatives from both the north and south supported protectionism because they believed a strong economy was vital to national sovereignty. Southern representatives viewed the use of protectionism as a "necessary evil."[20] At the same time, there was a faction in Congress that believed tariffs to support industry exceeded the powers of the federal government.[21]

It quickly became clear that the tariffs were not temporary. Their use was extended and even expanded in scope in order to in order to bolster the northern economy. With the Federal Government moving toward a seemingly never ending series of tariffs, a movement developed within several of the southern States in favor of disregarding federal law. One method discussed as early as 1820 was the use of a nullification act by a given State that would essentially make the federal tariff non-binding.

During the period of 1791–1821, South Carolinians came to believe that protectionism and the deliberate propping up of the northern economy was an oblique attack on the institution of slavery and the entire economic underpinnings of the south.[22] This belief that the northern controlled Congress would use economic means to abolish slavery put South Carolina in the greatest jeopardy. The ratio between slaves and free persons in South Carolina was greater than anywhere else in the south. Support for protectionism in the interest of the nation, began to evaporate. Popular opinion shifted toward a view that the tariff acts for were unconstitutional.

In 1832, an ordnance of nullification was adopted in the South Carolina Legislature. The new law declared the tariff acts of 1828 and 1832 "null, void and no law, nor binding upon this State, its officers or citizens."[23] The act, in effect, drew a line between the Union and South Carolina. Calhoun spoke of South Carolina "being driven out of the union," but offered an alternative that could allow the Federal Government to apply tariffs in South Carolina. The condition of applying tariffs was that they must be applied equally. The proposal did not allow the federal government to use tariffs to protect certain interests at the expense of others. Almost immediately President Andrew Jackson weighed in on the side of federalism and the preservation of the Union. In a public toast he declared, "our federal union-it must be preserved" only to be followed by Calhoun's "the Union, next our liberty most dear."

The conflict quickly developed into a more fundamental question than that of economic policy. It became an issue of States rights and the conditions under which membership in the Union was either sought or acquired. The movement by South Carolina was intended to demonstrate that local freedoms and self-determination outweighed the rule of the federal government, and that the State had the right to take itself out of the union.

The nullification crisis was resolved through a negotiated settlement in which a new tariff act was enacted that would drive down tariffs over a period of years. At the same time, legislation was enacted that reinforced the Federal right to impose and collect tariffs, despite the objection of a State.[24] This co-called "force bill," was enacted with the support of other southern States that did not line up behind South Carolina. South Carolina was isolated and chose to fall in line instead of risking a direct and possibly violent confrontation with the Union. As more laws and policies regarding trade were developed it became obvious that the southern lifestyle could not continue to exist in the Union, and that one possible course for southern aristocrats was secession. The choice to leave the Union would be delayed for almost thirty years, but a sectional rift had developed in 1832 that would eventually lead to civil war.

Secession, the Civil War and a State of Emergency

In its simplest sense the Civil War established that the Union and State membership in the Union was irrevocable. Until the secession of South Carolina and the other States the supremacy of the Union was not self-evident. For supremacy to be established, the North would have to win the Civil War. In the development of the Constitution there is little that would lead one to conclude that if a State chose to leave the Union they would no be permitted to do so. Nowhere in the Constitution is it specified that membership is irrevocable. That the United States would go to war to keep the Union intact was not clear in the period leading up to secession of the southern States. It is most significant that the federal government under President Lincoln did go to war and, in its prosecution, abused and even suspended constitutional rights and powers in the name of national crisis.

In May 1861, there was much concern as to whether Maryland would join the seceding States. President Lincoln and his Cabinet took measures they deemed appropriate to prevent Maryland public officials from leading a secession movement. Lincoln issued a directive to military commanders to suspend the Writ of Habeas Corpus for reasons explained nearly two months later in a Message to Congress. In the message, he included the following: "to arrest and detain without the ordinary process and forms of law…[anyone] considered dangerous to the public safety. This authority has been purposely exercised but sparingly."[25]

The decision by the President to suspend the writ of habeas corpus led to a confrontation with Supreme Court Chief Justice Roger B. Taney. In *Ex parte Merryman,* Taney ruled from the bench of the Maryland Circuit Court that the President had acted improperly in that the Constitution gave no authority to the President to suspend the writ.[26] Citing Article I, Section 9 which reads: "The privilege of the Writ of Habeas Corpus shall not be suspended, unless when in the case of Rebellion or Invasion the public Safety shall require it," Taney's argument was clear—that Article 1 of the Constitution describes the powers of the Congress, not the President.

Lincoln did not comply with the Chief Justice's order to grant the Writ of Habeas Corpus to Merryman. Instead he sought Congressional approval for his actions as Commander-in-Chief. When Congress convened, it issued a Joint Resolution supporting all actions of the President since the start of hostilities except the suspension of the writ of habeas corpus.[27] In another example of abuse of powers, General Dix issued an order in November 1861 during a Maryland election to arrest anyone that came to the polls suspected of supporting secession.[28]

During the civil war, clearly a time of national emergency, the President and his cabinet had numerous citizens arrested or detained, disrupted local elections and suppressed the First Amendment right by seizing and shutting down northern newspapers opposed to the war and often arresting the owners and employees.[29]

The fact that the Congress did not condemn the Presidents actions is a result of the belief that the security of the nation was at risk. In the case of the Civil War, the danger was visible, the emergency obvious and the President was given great latitude to deal with the crisis.

The actions of President Lincoln, Chief Justice Taney and the Congress represent that during a time of emergency or national crisis, the threshold for abuse of power is altered significantly. When the executive proclaims a threat to national security, he can undertake extreme measures in response to the threat that would usually not be tolerated. The relevance of this issue will become more important in the next chapter when addressing the use of declaration of a "state of emergency" by modern Presidents.

The Great Depression, The New Deal and Growth in Government

The Great Depression was a more recent period of major change in the relationship between the States and the Federal Government. An interesting note in the discussion of the effects of the Depression is the claim by economist Milton Friedman[30] that the primary cause of the depression was the creation of the Federal Reserve. If Friedman is correct in his conclusion, then the increase of federal powers to deal with a national emergency stem from an earlier increase in federal powers.[31]

In language that is often an indicator of new and expansive Federal Government operations Roosevelt used the phrase "war against the emergency" in his inaugural address.[32] The Presidential use of the phrase "war against emergency..." has historically provided the user with unprecedented power to expand government.[33]

The response to the depression by the Roosevelt Administration was to create a federal safety net for citizens adversely affected by the economic crisis. A massive expansion of government in the form of new regulatory agencies was a result of Roosevelt's plan for recovery. Much tighter regulatory restrictions were placed on the private sector and huge government employment programs were put in place. Much of today's domestic social policies can be traced to the policies instituted by the New Deal. Many of the initiatives changed the role of the central government. The Emergency Banking Act/Federal Deposit Insurance Corporation shifted the oversight of banks from local managers to federal inspectors. The Fair Labor Standards Act of 1938 banned child labor and established the minimum wage. The Social Security Act provide government managed old-age pensions, unemployment insurance and a myriad of disabilities related benefits for the workers of America.

At the outset of World War II, the United States had already seen a distinct shift in the roles of the States and the Federal Government. The nullification crisis established that States would not be able to selectively discard federal laws they believed to be inconsistent with a certain way of life; the secession of the southern States and the Civil War established that membership in the Union would be permanent, enforced by the Federal Government, and that during a crisis the President would wield broad powers; and the Great Depression provided the catalyst for the central government to move to regulate activities that had previously been reserved to the States.

The next section will discuss the ways in which the federal government itself has expanded. The tendency for authorities to move from the States to the federal government coincides, or led to, a commensurate expansion of powers in each of the branches. While the growth of each branch has its own peculiar method and result, they have all assumed greater roles when compared to the States.

Executive Branch Expansion

During the New Deal, the executive branch of the federal government grew in numbers of agencies and employees. By centralizing social services as national programs, the federal government has been able to exert greater influence in areas that are reserved to the States, such as influencing police powers and public safety issues. Presidential declarations have been used as a method to influence or control the actions of the States by linking compliance to the availability of funds.

The Executive Order is a mechanism used by the President to direct the daily operations of the government. Since the Hoover administration began in 1924, there have been 8,436 Executive Orders signed and entered into the Federal Register.[34] Most Executive Orders are administrative in nature and are limited to defining how the executive branch should function but they have occasionally been used as a mechanism to bypass the role of the Congress. An Executive Order was used by President Clinton to coerce states and companies into supporting union businesses by restricting the use of federal funds for contracts that used companies that had hired non-union workers during a strike. Clinton chose to use the Executive Order to direct the federal agencies to withhold funding because he could not get Congressional support for this initiative.[35] By using the power of the federal budget and the federal bureaucracy to force State compliance, Clinton was able to meet his objective without following any Constitutionally approved process. Most recently this mechanism was used to establish the Office of Homeland Security.

Another method by which the Executive can implement large-scale policy direction is through Presidential Directives on National Security. Since the Truman administration, every President has published a series of documents that, unlike the Executive Order, do not get published in the National Register.[36] The documents, which change in title from president to president are often classified and limited in distribution. These documents give the president the ability to put into action government programs that, as in the Executive Order, do not go through any legislative or judicial review. Moreover, they do not have to withstand public scrutiny. Presidential Directives on National Security range from the use of space[37] to a issuing a strategy to bring about the destruction of the Soviet Union.[38] This process has been generally the method of choice by all Presidents since Ronald Reagan in issuing policy on the government's preparations and response to terrorism.

Congressional Branch Change

Another shift in the balance of power between the States and the federal governments came with the passage of the Seventeenth Amendment in 1913. The method of appointing Senators changed from being selected by state legislatures to direct election by the people of each State. This had the effect of removing State governments from the process of selecting who would represent them in Washington and fundamentally changed the delicate balance described by Madison in Federalist 39. The process of selecting Senators did not evolve the way the Framers had envisioned, legislatures selecting the Senators based on superior public service and community standing. Instead, the development of political machines changed Senatorial appointments into political reward for fund-raising and other activities deemed important by party bosses.[39] While the decision to change the method of selecting Senators may have been appropriate, it did change the role of the Senate in a subtle way. No longer did the Senator need to concern himself with representing the interest of the State government, now he responded directly to the people of the State.

The growth of the power of Congress did not keep pace with the executive and the disparity between the two branches reached a critical point in 1974. In his book The Power Game, Hedrick Smith describes that year as "The Power Earthquake of 1974." He argues that the balance of power between the Executive and Legislative branches had leaned toward the executive in large part because of the growth of expertise in the executive branch. The Congress had to depend on experts in budgetary and technical matters from the Executive agencies, and became frustrated with the lack of congressional organizations that could provide independent verification of claims by the Executive. Frustration with Johnson's handling of the Vietnam War, and confrontations with Nixon over policies, led to Congress developing it own cadre of experts to assist in the execution of its constitutional role[40].

Congress created the Congressional Budget Office in 1974 that provided the members with an alternative to the budget projections put forth by the White House. Prior to this, Congress had to depend exclusively on the reports by the Office of Management and Budget. Congressional Staff had grown from 11,500 in 1973, to over 24,000 in 1986 and the number of House subcommittees peaked in 1975 at 172.[41] With this growth in the size and scope of Congressional organization came an equally startling growth in the number and breadth of lobbyist. In 1961, there were 365 lobbyist registered with Congress, and by 1987 there were 43,011.[42] The growth in Congressional staff and the influence of lobby groups has changed the way legislation is developed.

Congress now uses internal and external experts in banking, social services, defense, education, and a seemingly limitless list of other topics to research and draft legislation. Legislation is often drafted by "experts" representing various lobby or special interest groups and coordinated with congressional staff. Hearings are scheduled to provide a Congressional Record of the research of the staff and lobby groups by ensuring that those with interest in the proposed legislation have the opportunity to testify. In the development of the Domestic Preparedness Act of 1996, I participated in the development of legislation designed to enhance First Responder's[43] ability to respond to terrorism in the United States. That effort followed the now standard process of soliciting lobbyist inputs, holding hearings with testimony supporting the objective of the new legislation and finally seeking assistance in crafting the language of the legislation from lobby groups, some executive agencies and a small group of experts.[44]

The two significant changes that have taken place in the Congress relative to the States are the direct election of the Senate and the development of the lobby group as a mechanism for citizens to bypass local and State government and be heard in Washington. Both changes have made the Congress a more nationally representative body and have changed the focus of the Congress from its original role of international and interstate commerce and the common defense to body that is more focused on internal issues and the general welfare of the citizens.

Judicial Expansion of Authority

The Supreme Court has been the most stable branch of the federal government. That being said, the Court is the branch of government that has deviated the most from the intent of the Framers as articulated by Alexander Hamilton. In Federalist No. 78 Hamilton describes the judiciary as the "least dangerous" branch of the central government. His argument that the judiciary is unlikely to threaten the liberties of citizens is based on a perceived lack of power. Hamilton goes on to say "The judiciary, on the contrary, [compared to the legislature and the executive] has no influence over either the sword or the purse; no direction either of the strength or the wealth of the society; and can take no active resolution whatever."[45] As history has shown, Hamilton was profoundly incorrect when he claimed that the Court would be able to "take no active resolution."

Court activism has been defined as the courts not limiting themselves to an opinion but also including remedial action in its decisions. In The New Color Line, authors Paul Craig Roberts and Lawrence M. Stratton cite the Court's decision in Brown v. Board of Education of Topeka, Kansas as a point of demarcation when the Court changed from judicial review to judicial activism. In the Brown case, the Court heard arguments that segregation was a violation of the constitutional rights of Americans. While there can be little dispute that segregation is not good for the individual or the society, the Court strayed from strict interpretation of the law and directed the States to desegregate their schools based on sociological factors. The case was argued twice before the Court at the urging of Justice Frankfurter, who wanted to find segregation unconstitutional but did not have the legal or political support necessary in 1952.[46] In short, although seeking an appropriate outcome, desegregation, the Court strayed from a role of interpreting the law to one of making law.

In a later case, Spallone v. United States, the Court overturned a ruling by a lower Federal court that had the effect of directing elected officials in Yonkers, New York to vote to expend funds to remedy a housing segregation issue. In the Opinion of the Court, Chief Justice Rehnquist cited the "federal common law of legislative immunity, where we have emphasized that any restriction on a legislator's freedom undermines the 'public good' by interfering with the rights of people to representation in the democratic process."[47] In this case, the District and Circuit Courts both felt it appropriate for a judge to direct the outcome of a legislative process. The Supreme Court reversed with only a 5–4 majority. There are numerous cases since Brown where the courts have directed remedial action. Issues such as busing and equal education have all brought down intervention from the courts. On balance the outcome of judicial activism has been beneficial to citizens, the courts have assumed a role that is not specified in the Constitution and certainly not consistent with the intent of the Framers

Summary

First and foremost in the creation of the American Federal System, is the Framers' intent to retain the prerogatives of the States regarding all aspects of life except commerce and the common defense. Second, the Federal Government has grown in size and scope throughout our national history. The federal government increased in stature as a result of the nullification crisis and the Civil War and the prerogatives of the States diminished accordingly. The "war on the emergency" declared by Roosevelt provided the impetus to greatly expand the role of the federal government in protecting the general welfare of Americans. All three branches of the federal government have expanded their powers. The Court under John Marshall established the role of judicial review. In the Brown case the Court directed desegregation, not based on law, but instead on social arguments. The courts have continued on an activist trend for the last fifty years. Finally, the powers of the President have grown with the size of the government he manages. Through the use of presidential directives such as the Executive Order the president wields more authority in more areas, without Congressional or Judicial review. The following chapter will look at how the growth of the federal government, the intrusion into authorities that had been reserved to the States and the use of non-legislated mandates have been woven into a national program to combat and prevent domestic terrorism.

2

The Evolution of National Security Policy

The development of a national security policy in the United States has been hampered by the particular evolution of state and federal government and the resulting manner in which government has dealt with national security issues. Throughout American history, the federal government has developed capabilities to protect the national interest and to meet any threat to that interest at the border or from abroad. That American national security is tailored primarily to protecting the citizens from threats abroad stems from the original concept of a common defense. Defense of the nation from external threats, whether it is an invasion as in the War of 1812, or the attacks on US interests overseas, has left America unprepared for dealing with internal threats such as domestic terrorism incidents. In the aftermath of the September 11th, attacks by Islamic extremist of the Al Qaeda organization[48] the national government is developing more expertise within executive branch to address homeland security. The Office of Homeland Security, the creation of the Transportation Security Administration, the appointment of an Executive Assistant Director of the FBI for Counterterrorism, and the creation of the Office of Energy Assurance within the Department of Energy are some of the examples of the changing structure. The effectiveness of President Bush's initiative has been constrained by the experiences of his national security team, as well as by structures designed for a different set of problems. The United States has never created a domestic capability to effectively deal with public safety and crisis management through a systematic approach that includes local and state governments. Instead the national government has attempted to apply international security strategies and capabilities to domestic issues, without due consideration to the fundamental differences between operations conducted abroad and those conducted with the United States.

From "Common Defense" to "National Security"

The Framers sought to place in the hands of a central government the powers required for the common defense of the new nation. The words "common defense" are representative of the idea that a national role would be the security of the states combined, not of individual states. This distinction is important in understanding that internal state security remained an issue for the state itself, not one for the national government. In Federalist 2, John Jay describes the benefit of a common defense managed by a national government.[49] He argues that with the security of the nation a national governmental function, the United States is best protected from external threats. Additionally, that a strong central government provides a moderating force for individual state disagreements, preventing minor interstate disputes from escalating into armed confrontation. By using the example of Spain cutting off access to the Mississippi, or Britain the Saint Lawrence, Jay makes the case for both strength and moderation. If the states bordering the Mississippi or Saint Lawrence were not part of a larger nation, they would be left on their own to deal with Spain or England in a territorial freedom-of-navigation dispute. Without a common defense, the states in question could not be assured of support from other states would not be strong enough to respond. Conversely, without the moderation of a central government Jay argued that individual states might enter into action against another government without consideration to the impact on the Union as a whole.

The security of the nation is measured alongside ability of the national government to preserve the principle of self-determination. Simply put, the national government has the obligation to ensure that the rights guaranteed in the Constitution continue uninterrupted. For the national government to meet its security obligation to the people it must have the strength to prevent internal or external threats from infringing upon the rights of its citizenry. The Constitution provides for the President to be the Commander-in-Chief to lead in time of war or conflict, and provides for a formal process by which the Congress overseas the scope and nature of armed conflict. The authorities delegated to the national government by the people provided sufficient powers to protect the nation from external threats as well against internal insurrection.

The Constitution does place absolute control over the armed forces in either the Executive or the Congress. Having been subjected to the imposition of tyrannical rule by a standing army, the Framers were careful to ensure that it would take both the Legislature and the executive to raise and employ an army. In Federalist 26, Hamilton outlines the checks and balances considered by the Framers when attempting to ensure an army could not be raised and maintained without justifiable cause.[50] Article I, Section 8 of the Constitution states that the legislature has the power "to raise and support Armies, but no appropriation of money to that use shall be for a longer term than two years." The wisdom of this language is that it provides for a permanent army to ensure preservation of the national security, under the control of a Commander-in-Chief, but requires Congress to annually or biannually review the need for the an army.

In the decades following independence the United States, military weakness threatened the national security. The United States did not gain independence from Great Britain due to military might. Had France not actively supported the American Revolution certainly would not have ended with Cornwallis' surrender in Yorktown. As a result the United States, although independent, did not receive the deference accorded a sovereign for many years. Two significant actions took place in 1801 and 1812 that would solidify the need for a standing army and navy in the United States. First was the determination by President Jefferson, an opponent to a standing military, to send ships to seek out and destroy the Barbary Pirates that had been raiding US commercial ships[51]. This was the first military expedition in which the United States attempted to influence its national security through projection of force. The next test of the United States' national security was a British invasion. The War of 1812 was the result of British refusal to respect America's right to free trade on the high seas. Britain routinely seized American vessels and captured seaman they claimed to be British citizens. The resulting invasion was a direct result of American military weakness.

The incidents ended the debate regarding a need for a standing federal army and navy. Standing military units were organized under the President and his Secretary of War.[52] The need for the application of military force to defend the borders and protect US interests abroad has been demonstrated on a regular basis over the last two hundred years. A strong standing military has become a commonly accepted requirement for the national government to meet its common defense responsibilities.

Once an internationally respected military was established, the United States began to use the projection of force as part of its foreign policy. The national government has been engaged in military operations abroad from the 1820s to the present.[53] Some of the overseas operations were major engagements such as World War I, World War II and the Spanish American War. Many others were smaller campaigns. All had a similar characteristic however: the fight was taken to foreign shores. The United States was not developing capabilities or a baseline of experience in national security within the borders. Military and intelligence related operations were aimed at other countries in foreign lands.

As the United States expanded its interests and influence over a wider span of the globe, its national security policies and structures remained relatively static for an extended period of time. There was no significant change in national security structure until 1947, when Congress and the President agreed that intelligence and war-making capabilities had grown to a size that required a new management structure.

The National Security Act of 1947

The National Security Act of 1947 was the first major piece of legislation to treat the mission and organization of defense, intelligence and diplomacy as a single cohesive process. The Act was required at the end of World War II in order to establish a formal structure that could oversee and coordinate the vast security complex that evolved during the war. Prior to and during World War II the conduct of international affairs, in particular as related to security was conducted in an ad-hoc manner. The Secretary of War and the Secretary of the Navy were of equal rank with the Secretary of State and policy influence was based as much on force of personality as it was doctrine.

The development of a National Security Council provided structure to the conduct of foreign policy, made up of defense, intelligence and diplomatic activities. The Council was made up of the newly created Secretary of Defense, the Secretary of State, and was chaired by the President. In addition to a National Security Council the Act established the Central Intelligence Agency. Significant for the purposes of this analysis is that in the creation and the subsequent evolution of the National Security Council there is little concern for issues of domestic security. National Security, even after the 1947 reorganization, has been almost exclusively restricted to international affairs and the capabilities of the traditional national security agencies, Defense, State and the CIA, reflect that focus.

The restriction of national security programs and objectives to international affairs precluded any substantive role for the states. Unlike the first century of the republic when the states would have played an important role by providing or withholding militia to support national objectives, even the control of the militia was transferred to the national government. The creation of a National Guard under the control of the President was proposed as early as 1863. A National Guard subject to the direction of the President, over the authority of the governors, would fundamentally shift power from the States to the Federal Government. In 1903, Congress finally passed legislation that created the National Guard, made up of the State militias and under the control of the federal government. Since 1903 the militia has been a reserve component of the Army, no longer under the control of the governors of the states.

Law Enforcement and National Security

The Federal Bureau of Investigation, as the law enforcement arm of the Justice Department has been the agency responsible for internal security since 1908.[54] The involvement of a federal law enforcement agency involved in national security can be traced back to 1917 when the Bureau assumed responsibility for espionage and acts of sabotage.[55] As the agency responsible for internal security the FBI has grown in size and scope. The FBI mission is clearly articulated in the Statute at Large[56] and on the FBI web page as follows: "The Mission of the FBI is to uphold the law through the investigation of violations of federal criminal law; to protect the United States from foreign intelligence and terrorist activities; to provide leadership and law enforcement assistance to federal, state, local, and international agencies; and to perform these responsibilities in a manner that is responsive to the needs of the public and is faithful to the Constitution of the United States.[57]" Included in the current mission of the FBI is the language "to protect the United States from foreign intelligence and terrorist activities." This protection is managed within the context of investigating violations of criminal law; therefore in order to take action to prevent a terrorist event the FBI has had to do so within the framework established by the Congress in defining criminal law. In order for the FBI to effectively prevent terrorism they must have a legislative mandate that specifies prevention as a responsibility in addition to the current authority to investigate crimes.

The Changing Threat

From the end of World War II until 1989 the United States had the luxury of maintaining a national security policy that was relatively static. The primary threat to the United States was perceived as the spread of communism and the imposition of totalitarian rule. The Truman doctrine established a policy of containment for the United States and all national security activities were in support of that policy. The evolution of a bi-polar world in which the United States and the Soviet Union were unambiguous opponents provided stability and simplified planning.

During this period the national security organizations previously discussed focused on prevention of the spread of terrorism abroad. International terrorism was considered criminal activity, not warfare and therefore was dealt with differently from the real threat, the Soviet Union.[58] As discussed in the opening chapter, Presidents have used executive orders and other Presidential directives to organize the executive when dealing with national security. Until the crisis resulting from the September 11, 2001 attacks Presidents dealt with terrorism within a national security apparatus that was designed to prevent the spread of communism abroad or as part of a criminal investigation. Virtually all specific policy for preventing and responding to acts of terrorism have been promulgated as Presidential directives. The following section provides an overview of the evolution of terrorism policy within the executive branch.

Terrorism and National Security

Counterterrorism, as a policy issue, has been on the agenda of each President since Richard Nixon. Immediately following the 1972 Munich Olympics massacre, President Nixon directed his National Security Advisor to develop a US policy for dealing with terrorism. The policy put in place during the Nixon Administration was principally one of high-level monitoring and observation. There was no plans developed that would include military or diplomatic action to prevent or deter terrorism. Nixon developed a Cabinet Committee on Terrorism that met only once during the Nixon and Ford Administrations, and was eventually disbanded in 1977.[59] The Carter Administration did not put any emphasis on terrorism until the Iran Hostage Crisis, after which, a new policy structure was put in place. President Carter established a Cabinet level coordinating committee and several subordinate groups to coordinate federal agency activities and share information. President Carter also directed the Federal Bureau of Investigation, the Federal Aviation Administration and the State Department to be the lead agencies to manage the federal response to terrorism. He delineated responsibilities for response to terrorism by establishing command and control relationships and directing other agencies such as Defense and Energy to operate in support (subordinate to) the established lead agencies. This is the first time leadership responsibilities were specifically assigned to the FBI to act a lead federal agency to address domestic terrorism.[60]

During the Reagan administration the United States first started to deal with terrorist attacks against US interests abroad.[61] President Ronald Reagan signed the first policy directive issued by the Reagan Administration on terrorism on 10

April 1982. In NSDD-10, Reagan refined the management protocols that President Carter had put in place by further defining the roles of the FBI and the State Department as lead federal agencies. The Reagan administration structure for the management of a terrorist incident remained in placed until the September 11th attack on the World Trade Center and the Pentagon. While there was some minor modification to the structure that Reagan set up in 1982 the basic concept under which the federal government would manage terrorism incidents has remained one of a "lead agency" approach. The Federal Bureau of Investigation is the lead agency for domestic incidents, the State Department for International Incidents and the Federal Aviation Administration for aircraft hijackings.

The Collapse of the Soviet Union and a New "Emergency"

The collapse of the Soviet Union in 1989 and the threat of proliferation of Weapons of Mass Destruction created a new challenge for George Bush and Bill Clinton. As the bipolar world of Soviet-Western political blocs dissipated a power vacuum was created. During the Cold War, most state sponsored terrorism was overseen by foreign intelligence organizations such as the KGB and the CIA. How one views a particular political struggle often determines whether an act of violence is terrorism or unconventional warfare conducted by freedom fighters.[62] During the Cold War the United States and the Soviet Union used unconventional warfare, or terrorism, as part of a larger foreign policy. The use of terrorism through surrogate groups provided for a level of control that was lost with the collapse of the Soviet Union. This loss of control and the threat of weapons of mass destruction changed the dynamics of the terrorist threat.

Terrorism plans and policies in the post Cold War Era, prior to September 11, 2001, remained basically unchanged despite significant increases in threats and a change in the geopolitical environment. George H. W. Bush kept in place the Reagan structure and plans for combating terrorism. No formal policy changes or direction were promulgated during the Bush Administration. This is not surprising when one considers that Bush had been Reagan's Vice President and in that position was responsible for crafting terrorism related policy. The Bush foreign policy team was focused on the Gulf War in the immediate aftermath of the Soviet collapse and did not adjust terrorism policy to deal with the emerging threats. In 1992 President Clinton came to power in a world unlike that of his predecessors. Unfortunately, Clinton was extremely slow to act regarding the proliferation of nuclear materials and the availability of those materials to terrorist. When he did finally act his policies did not sufficiently address the changing and growing threat.

In November 1994 Clinton signed Executive Order 12938 which reads in part, "I WILLIAM J. CLINTON, President of the United States of America, find that the proliferation of nuclear, biological, and chemical weapons, ("weapons of mass destruction") and the means of delivering such weapons, constitutes an unusual and extraordinary threat to the national security, foreign policy, and economy of the United States, and hereby declare a national emergency to deal with that threat."[63] The actions directed by Clinton as part of this Executive Order were focused on commerce and economic activities; there is no mention of actions by any Defense or National Security Agency. While Clinton articulated the threat in Executive Order 12938, he took no action to effectively deal with it at that time. In June of 1995 Clinton issued Presidential Decision Directive 39, much of which remains classified. PDD-39 was the Clinton Administration's first attempt at a national counterterrorism policy and provides direction for a well-rounded program. PDD-39 addressed the reduction of vulnerabilities abroad and within the United States, efforts to deter terrorism as well as respond to acts of terrorism and includes weapons of mass destruction policies.

PDD-39 deviates from precedents in the management of domestic incidents by assigning the lead agency responsibility for crisis resolution[64] to the FBI and the responsibility for Consequences Management (or disaster recovery) to FEMA. This change is significant, for the first time FEMA was assigned a lead role in the response to terrorism within the United States. This assignment took advantage of legislation that already gave FEMA broad authorities to assist the states in time of crisis, something that was not the case with the FBI.

Up until this point all discussion on terrorism policy has focused on the use of Presidential Directives, some during a state of emergency. Unlike Lincoln and Roosevelt's use of emergency powers and executive authority being followed up by detailed legislation, terrorism policy has been mostly exclusive of the legislative process.

Until the 104th Congress there was no substantive legislation that dealt with responding to terrorism in the United States.[65] The interest of the Congress with respect to domestic terrorism was virtually non-existent prior to the World Trade Center Bombing in 1993 and did not intensify until after the Oklahoma City bombing and the sarin gas attack in Tokyo in 1995. Since 1995 the Congress has taken a much more proactive approach in terrorism legislation, directing federal assistance to states and assigning statutory responsibilities to several executive agencies. Representative Ike Skelton of South Carolina requested the General

Accounting Office review the executive branch efforts to combat terrorism in 1997. Rep. Skelton's request has resulted in a series of documents that provide the Congress with an independent assessment of counterterrorism activities within the executive branch. This detailed analysis by the GAO has provided the Congress the opportunity to become more engaged in the oversight of terrorism related programs that had traditionally been managed through internal classified National Security Directives. Despite this increase in Congressional interest there is still no legislation that addresses the balance of power and the appropriate roles of the states and the national government when dealing with the crisis phase of a terrorist event.

In summing up chapter two we have seen that the national security structure and policies of the United States have evolved in a manner that makes internal security protection extremely difficult and completely bypasses the States in the protection of citizens. As the Commander in Chief the President has used the Executive Order and National Security Directives to cause the executive branch to undertake internal security responsibilities without legislative mandate. The most casual observer would now agree that the original intent of the Framers to limit the powers of the President through two-year military appropriations is obsolete. Virtually every Congressional district benefits from military spending and the idea that the Congress with move to cease funding the military is wholly unrealistic. While the Congress has passed legislation freeing the military to provide support to the civil sector it is limited to special skills and capabilities developed for the conduct of warfare overseas. National security capabilities and tactics developed for warfare are adapted for domestic use, not developed for domestic use.[66] Additionally, the Presidential directives direct the national law enforcement structure to lead government efforts to deter and respond to terrorism. The FBI, in its role as lead federal agency does not respond to a request from a state for assistance in this role. Rather, the FBI is in charge of the effort. This Presidential requirement for the FBI to act in a lead role when public safety is an overriding consideration puts it at odds with state emergency managers and is an expansion of national government powers without due process since there is no legislative mandate for the FBI to direct multi-agency responses, the Congressional mandate to the FBI is only to investigate crimes.

The problems associated with the FBI taking charge of a domestic crisis without a request from the state, or a requirement to inform the state that an operation is underway risks conflicts between the various levels of government at the worst possible time, that is, during a crisis. It is during a crisis that all branches and levels of government must be able to work quickly and effectively to ensure that the crisis can be resolved without escalating into a disaster such as the detonation of a terrorist nuclear device.

As discussed in the opening chapter the national government has tremendous capabilities to assist the states in resolving such a crisis and the FBI is best suited to lead a national effort. However, the FBI should lead that effort in support of a State Governor, not at the exclusion of local authorities. As the lead federal agency the FBI has the ability to draw on military and other national security resources while operating within the restrictions of the Constitution.

The following chapter will discuss the problems associated with efforts to protect the public through national legislation as well as providing an analysis of a very successful law tailored to assist states in times of emergency which provides a model for crisis operations.

3

Limitations on Federal Regulation of Public Safety

The first two chapters of this paper have laid the groundwork for a discussion on the role of Congress in legislating the response to domestic terrorism. The steady movement of powers from the states to the national government has created a situation that has effectively removed the states from the decision making process and restricted the ability of the Governors and state legislatures to exercise police powers. In addition, the tendency of the Executive to utilize presidential directives to regulate the response to terrorism has limited the role of Congress in developing national policy in this important area of national security. Unlike the management in previous crises when a president signed emergency declarations and Congress followed up with legislation, current counterterrorism policies have not undergone congressional scrutiny nor has there been a serious effort to codify terrorism response plans in federal law.

As of this writing, virtually all directives regarding the response to terrorism are presidential documents that have not been followed up with changes to law or the Constitution. Presidential Decision Directive 39, addressed in the previous chapter provides an example of a document that assigned responsibility to the Federal Bureau of Investigation to manage incidents within the States but makes no mention of how the State fits in. A debate in Congress about role of the Federal Government, as defined in PDD-39, and the impact of that role on the States' ability to protect the public is warranted. If the Congress finds the policy to be consistent with the Constitution is should become the law of the land.

The national plans for responding to terrorism are divided into two distinct categories: crisis and consequences.[67] The crisis phase is the period in which actions would be undertaken by national response teams to prevent the successful completion of a terrorist act. The second phase of response, consequences, is the post attack recovery, referred to in national plans as the consequences management phase.

An example of the distinction between the two phases is provided by the terrorist acts of September 11, 2001. As soon as the aircraft were hijacked the lead federal agency for crisis resolution was the Federal Aviation Administration, after the planes crashed FEMA would become the lead federal agency to assist the states in recovery operations.

Another example would be the use of a large bomb, or a weapon of mass destruction in the United States. Should the national government learn of a plot to detonate such a device the Federal Bureau of Investigation would lead the federal effort to locate and disarm the device before it could be detonated. In this context it is better to look at the phases of operations as prevention and recovery with the separation point being the detonation of a bomb or the crashing of an aircraft when preventive actions are no longer applicable.

The major distinction in the management of the crisis and consequences phases is that the consequence phase is undertaken with statutory authorities that require federal assistance to the state, in direct support of the governor, while the crisis phase is covered by very little specific statutory authority and is not undertaken in support of the state. Since the crisis phase has no statutory authorities it also has no statutory limitations. With no defined legal limits, the FBI could conduct crisis operations within a state without notifying the governor of that state that there is a significant threat to the citizens.

In the management of domestic terrorist incidents the evolution of national policy has led to federal employees deciding when the priorities of an agency outweigh the States' need to protect the public. This situation is in conflict with the Constitution because it allows the federal government to define the scope of its own authorities. The current policy does not represent the consent of the governed, the representatives of the people have not voted on whether it is appropriate for a federal agency such as the FBI to directly manage incidents involving public safety without due deference to the states. The Constitution has not been amended to delegate the authority to prevent, through active engagement, a terrorist incident by national assets without informing the state.

This chapter will address the difficulty in legislating national police powers through the analysis of two federal laws that were designed to enhance public safety. The first deals with preventing the use or possession of weapons in schools. The Gun-Free School Zones Act of 1990 was a law that sought to make it illegal to possess a gun within one thousand feet of a school anywhere in the United States. The Congress used the powers of the commerce clause of the Constitution as the basis for the authority to regulate the possession of guns. One could easily understand the rationale for such a law, attempting to make schools safer for children by proscribing the presence of weapons in or near a school. However, when challenged in the Supreme Court the Gun Free School Zone Act was found to exceed the authority of the Congress.

Lopez: A Case of Exceeding Federal Authority

The case of *United States v. Lopez*[68] provides an excellent example of how the Congress can, in an effort to enhance public safety, exceed its authority. Lopez, a student in San Antonio, Texas had been tried and convicted under a federal statute, the Gun-Free School Zone Act of 1990. The conviction was overturned by the Court of Appeals for the Fifth Circuit. The Supreme Court upheld that decision finding that Congress had exceeded the authority delegated to it in the Constitution.

The issue before the Court in the *Lopez* case was whether a seemingly isolated criminal act has a connection to commerce strong enough to justify the Congress passing a nationally enforced law. There is precedent for congressional action connecting criminal activity and commerce. The Lindbergh Law, enacted to make kidnapping a federal offense is an example of a less than obvious connection. The Lindbergh Law, despite being a law that was written with public safety and law enforcement in mind, showed a relationship to the commerce clause by specifying that the law applied to interstate criminal activity. The Mann Act, also known as the White Slavery Act, was passed to prevent the transport of persons across state lines for illegal purposes. The Mann Act, as did the Lindbergh Law explicitly identified interstate activity as the basis for the legislation, thus ensuring a direct linkage to the Constitutional authority of Congress under the Commerce Clause. The text of the legislation before the Court in *Lopez* did not include any language regarding interstate activity nor did it include any reference to commerce.

A brief history of the case and the events leading up to the constitutional challenge follows. In March 1992 a student at Edison High School in San Antonio, Texas was arrested for carrying a concealed weapon on school grounds. He was charged under Texas law with firearms possession on school premises. The following day, Texas authorities dropped the state charges after Lopez was charged with violating 18 USC 922, the Gun Free School Zone Act of 1990. The Texas state law and the Federal statute were not in conflict since the text of the federal statute includes language that is supportive of local and state laws prohibiting the possession of firearms. It would appear that Lopez could have been convicted under the state law without incident but when the US Attorney chose to invoke the federal statute the State of Texas deferred and dropped the state charges. The Supremacy Clause of the Constitution[69] provides that when Congress has provided legislation regarding a particular issue the regulation of that issue becomes a federal responsibility. The State governments cannot enforce laws that are contrary to the federal statute nor, as discussed in the section on nullification, can they block the enforcement of that statute. Although the legislation in question does not proscribe states from enacting similar legislation it does provide for federal supremacy in enforcement of the Act. In this case the Texas law was not contrary to the federal statue and there appears to be no need for federal action.

Lopez was indicted by a federal grand jury for violating the federal statute. He then sought immediate dismissal of the charges, claiming that the law itself was unconstitutional. Lopez claimed that the Congress did not have the power to legislate control over public schools. The District Court denied the motion for dismissal, stating that the law "is a constitutional exercise of Congress' well defined power to regulate activities in and affecting commerce, and the 'business of elementary, middle and high schools...affects interstate commerce."[70]Following his failure to have the charges dismissed, Lopez waived his right to trial and was convicted by the District Court. Upon appeal he challenged the conviction, claiming that the law in question exceeds Congress's Constitutional authority under the commerce clause. The Court of Appeals for the Fifth Circuit reversed the conviction sighting insufficient Congressional findings and legislative history. The Supreme Court accepted the case under a writ of certiorari. Lopez did not try to argue guilt or innocence throughout the process, the case to go before the Court was to determine if Congress exceeded its authority in creating the law.

The law itself was common sense legislation. Congress recognized that guns in schools were creating an unhealthy environment for children and developed legislation to prohibit such action. The Gun Free School Zones Act of 1990 was introduced in the House on November 20, 1989. The Act sought to make it "unlawful for any individual to knowingly possess a firearm at a place that the individual knows, or has reasonable cause to believe, is a school zone." The Act specifies that it does not preempt or prevent a State or local government from enacting a statute establishing gun-free school zones, thus allowing States to create or retain laws that would provide for prosecution of such offenses. The Act defines the punishment and specifies the US Code[71] to be modified by the Act. The bill was sent to the House Judiciary Committee for legislative action; only one hearing took place on the legislation, before the House Subcommittee on

Crime[4]. It was passed by both houses without floor debate and signed into law by the President. In the legislative process there was no direct reference to the commerce clause although that relationship was the basis for the government's claim that the law was valid. By signing the bill into law without seeking the Congress provide language connecting the law to Constitutional authority, the President did not exercise his right to check this expansion of federal powers.

The US Constitution delegates the authority for Congress to regulate commerce. Article I Section 8 states that "The Congress shall have the power to regulate commerce with foreign nations, and among the several States, and with Indian tribes." This clause seems relatively straightforward, explicitly defining the Congress' powers to be restricted to commerce that affects more than one state or between a state and another country. It does not provide authority to regulate intrastate commerce nor does it address public safety or police powers. In Federalist 42 Madison describes the commerce clause as a remedy to the interstate commerce restrictions that resulted for the Articles of Confederacy. Madison stresses responsibilities that can only be managed by a central government and the examples he gives are directly tied to trade. He gives the examples: to coin money and regulate the value thereof; to standardize weights and measures; to establish a uniform rule of naturalization, and uniform laws of bankruptcy; to prescribe the manner in which public acts, records and judicial proceedings of each State shall be proved; and the effect they shall have in other States; and to establish post offices and post roads. Madison establishes the ties between a central government and commerce and provides examples that detail why, under a Confederacy, the government is ineffective in regulating commerce. He makes the case that Congressional regulation of commerce is beneficial to the nation as a whole. Madison argues that the regulation of interstate commerce is clearly a federal function if the United States function and be perceived as one nation.[72] One example of authority under the commerce clause that stands out in light of the Lopez case is his reference to the punishment for counterfeiting. By claiming for the Congress the authority to provide for criminal punishment in the case of counterfeiting Madison ties the criminal prosecution of laws affecting commerce to the commerce clause. The logic used by Madison in this case is that the Federal Government produces the currency and establishes the value thereof. If money is counterfeited and distributed the value of the money will be affected, thereby directly effecting commerce. It is clear from Madison's writing of Federalist 42 that criminal prosecutions of acts effecting interstate commerce were considered by the framers to be within the Congress' authority.

Chief Justice Rehnquist wrote the Opinion of the Court in *US v. Lopez*. In a detailed review the Chief Justice describes the "principles" by which the Congress has authority to enact law. Quoting Madison from Federalist 45 "the powers delegated by the proposed Constitution to the federal government are few and defined. Those which are to remain in the State governments numerous and indefinite." He describes the history of the Court and the commerce clause in order to establish three categories in which the Congress has authority to regulate. First, "Congress may regulate the use of the channels of interstate commerce;" second, "the Congress has the power to regulate and protect the instrumentalities of interstate commerce, or persons or things in interstate commerce, even though the threat may come only from interstate activities." And, finally "Congress' commerce authority includes the power to regulate those activities having a substantial relation to interstate commerce." In determining whether Congress has exceeded its powers the Court must determine if the Congress acted under any of the three broad categories.

Rehnquist immediately dismisses the first two categories in this case and therefore if law is to be upheld it must therefore be proven to substantially affect interstate commerce. The Chief Justice reviews several cases in which the Court upheld Congressional acts regulating interstate economic activity where the Court concluded that the activity substantially affects interstate commerce. All but one of the cases cited were directly tied to interstate commerce by operating either across state lines, serving patrons from other states or producing a product for sale in another state. The only case he mentions that was not directly tied to interstate commerce was *Wickard v. Filburn*. Although Rehnquist refers to *Wickard* as "perhaps the most far reaching example of Commerce Clause authority" he finds that there was a direct tie between the amount of wheat produced by a private farmer and the federal governments efforts to control wheat prices to ensure a stable national economy. He makes the point at this time that carrying a gun in school does not affect the economy in any like manner.

Rehnquist states that 18 USC 922(q) is a criminal statute and has nothing to do with commerce or the economy. He points out that the section of the law is not a part of a larger economic act of which it is an integral part and therefore cannot be upheld as a regulation substantially affecting interstate commerce. He reviews the government argument that guns in a school zone constitute a violent crime, which will affect the economy. The government contends that since violent crimes create a greater insurance burden there is a direct economic tie and further argues that areas with high rates of violent crime hinder interstate travel, thus restricting a right of all citizens to unfettered interstate travel. The government also contends that violence in the schools leads to less effective legislation and therefore less productive citizens who will adversely affect productivity and therefore the national economy. The Chief Justice warns that by demonstrating that any type of crime creates high costs, and thereby effects the economy, the government would be free to regulate almost every crime as impacting the economy and therefore subject to the commerce clause. If the Congress has the authority to regulate activities that affect educational efficiency and the potential productivity of students it would stand to reason that the Congress could claim authority over curriculum and virtually any other school activity that has effect on the quality of education.

Rehnquist concluded that although Congress has the authority to enact legislation that substantially affects interstate commerce, the government had not shown a direct linkage in this case; rather, the Congress strayed into the realm of police powers, which are reserved for the States by attempting to connect criminal activity to commerce.

Justice Thomas wrote a separate concurring opinion in which he argued that the Congress and the Court far exceeded what the framers intended for the Federal control of commerce. Thomas points out that by adding a "substantial effect" test the Court allows the federal government to assume a police power role with ambiguous limits. He makes the point early in his opinion that the majority and Justice Breyer, who dissents in this case, are in agreement that the Federal Government has no police power authority. This point, repeated by the justices, is extremely important in answering the question of how to legislate about a response to terrorism. By keying on the "substantial effect" language that the Court has sanctioned in past cases, Justice Thomas discusses a type of domino effect that could allow all aspects of life to be consumed by the application of a "substantial effect" test. Thomas provides a very narrow interpretation of the commerce clause, arguing that the Framers defined commerce as buying, selling, bartering and the transportation of products. He reviews Hamilton's writings that specified commerce was separate from other economic actions such as manufacture and agriculture and therefore commerce and the legislation of commerce should be limited to the actual exchange of goods as opposed to virtually anything related to commerce. The point is made that by allowing the interpretation of the commerce clause to include actions that effect commerce the Court is negating the rest of Article I Section 8. Thomas continues that by allowing a very liberal interpretation of the clause the Congress begins to usurp the power and authority of the States. The authority that resides with the Congress is to regulate national concerns, leaving local concerns to the States to regulate, the Constitution did not grant the Congress the authority to regulate everything it deems to be national. The Constitution is very clear in the enumerated powers and Thomas believes that the Court must rethink the "substantial effect" test to eliminate additional authorities being derived from the actual enumerated powers. Thomas uses a rather extreme example of the result of an overly broad interpretation of the clause, stating that under the current thinking the Congress could pass an omnibus "substantially affects interstate commerce" statute that could regulate all aspects of human existence. While Thomas's arguments end being extreme, the logic by which he reaches his conclusion is sound. There is no language in the Constitution that allows the Federal government to expand its authority past the powers specifically delegated by the States. If Congress could add modifiers throughout the text of the Constitution that allowed laws only be related to the specified authorities there is unlimited room for Federal intrusion into everyday life. Thomas concurs that the law exceeded Congress' authority but does not support the majority view that if there had been a direct connection between guns in school and a substantial affect on commerce the law would be constitutional.

Justice Kennedy wrote an opinion concurring with the invalidation of the law but added some additional concerns relating to Congress attempting to regulate public safety at the local level. Kennedy discusses the first hundred years of the Court's work on commerce clause cases as providing limitations on State restrictions on commerce as opposed to reviewing Congressional activity. He, like Thomas, sees a difference between the interstate movement of goods and the manufacturing process. The latter is more difficult to accept as Federal since the process of manufacture may reside entirely within the borders of a state. Kennedy does not take issue with the "substantial effect" test that Thomas would remove but instead discusses the balance of power and checks and balances between the States and the Federal government. He points out that commerce in the eighteenth century and commerce today are very different and therefore the role of the Congress should be very different. The existence of a single market and a national economy, that must be kept stable,[73] gives Congress a broader set of authorities than Thomas would concede, since the several States are connected in almost all forms of commercial enterprise. Kennedy believes the entire commercial sphere is within the Congress' authority to regulate. The point that Kennedy seems to be making regarding the Congressional authority under the commerce clause is that an explicate reference to interstate commerce is no longer required. The fact that the commercial sphere is itself interstate in nature all commerce is inter-related and therefore part of a national economy subject to Federal oversight.

Despite his relatively liberal interpretation of the commerce clause, Kennedy is not ready to concede that the Federal government can extend that sphere to include criminal activity. He does not agree that the possession of a firearm in a school (or within 1000 feet) is in any way a commercial activity He makes it clear that the responsibility for the safety and welfare of the schools resides with the States. The point that the federal government cannot practically enforce such a law or tailor punishment to the community needs is made. Kennedy highlights the problem of federal control over this type of activity by maintaining that mere are now over 100,000 schools with an imaginary 1000-foot federal zone around it. Each of those zones, despite the location and demographics has the same restriction. Local authorities drafting laws tailored to their needs would provide for greater flexibility and more efficient enforcement. He also points out that at the time the Federal law was passed over forty States already had similar laws in place. Kennedy concludes that the Gun Free School Zones Act is an intrusion on state sovereignty and exceeds the authority of Congress for that reason, not because of a relationship to the commerce clause.

The justices differed in this case on the limits of the commerce clause and the latitude that should be given the Congress to regulate commerce. However, they agreed that the Gun Free Schools Zone Act was flawed because it actually regulated police powers and public safety, not commerce. If the objective of a law is to regulate public safety through police powers, the authority to do so rests with the state, not the federal government.

The Lopez decision provides some challenges for congressional policy makers in assessing the potential impact on federal intervention into law enforcement issues.

There are many laws on the books that could easily be construed as police power regulations that should reside within die State. For example, the Defense Against Weapons of Mass Destruction Act of 1996[74] is one such law that has not been challenged in the courts. The law gives federal agencies the authority to enter a State and take charge of any terrorist activity or activity that may involve a nuclear, chemical or biological device. While the argument has been made that the federal government unique assets and expertise that can assist locals in protecting the citizens the law does not require any request for that assistance from the locals.[75] A criminal prosecuted under this Act with the federal agencies acting in a public safety role, preempting State and local laws may find himself in the same situation as Lopez. He may be guilty of a criminal act but not convicted because of the federal government attempting to regulate and enforce laws that are within the purview of the States.

The Lopez decision places restrictions on congressional mandates that would standardize criminal prosecution and punishment. Justice Kennedy's description of the federal government enacting a law with 100,000 new federally restricted zones is indicative of the problems facing Congress with respect to laws affecting public safety. This case also brings into light the dilemma of the State in deferring to Federal Government to create and enforce laws that may be challenged and overturned in the Courts. Had the State of Texas simply prosecuted Lopez he would have been punished according to State and local laws, instead the State deferred to the Federal government and justice was not served. The consequences of States depending on the Congress to pass laws that are criminal in nature and only loosely tied to Constitutional authorities such as the commerce clause are broad. If the State does not prosecute criminals under State law they risk the same result has happened with *Lopez*.

Lopez provides an example of a case where either the state or the federal government had the capability to protect public safety through law enforcement. In the case where either level of government is equally capable, the power should reside at the lowest level. When the ability of the state to protect the public is exceeded, national plans should provide a means for assistance. The following discussion will introduce a law that is designed to provide federal resources to protect the public in a way that respects the powers reserved to the states.

The Stafford Act: Proper Application of Federal Assistance

The Disaster Relief Act[76] was passed by the 93rd Congress and signed into law on May 22 1974. Section 101 (b) reads "It is the intent of the Congress, by this Act, to provide an orderly and continuing means of assistance by the Federal Government to State and local governments in carrying out their responsibility to alleviate the suffering and damage which result from such disasters"[77] The Congress makes very clear in the Findings and Declarations of the Act that it is the responsibility of the States to alleviate suffering and damages, not the responsibility of the national government.

The programs established by the Stafford Act include federal assistance to prepare for and mitigate the affects of a disaster, provide training and exercise assistance, and the application of science and technology. This assistance is provided in the form of grants to the states following an application by the Governor. The legislation also requires that the federal government provide assistance in developing warning capabilities and that it provide warning to the states. Emergency assistance to "save lives and protect property and public health and safety" may be provided by the President upon receipt of a request from the Governor of an affected state.

During an emergency the President directs the Federal Emergency Management Agency to activate the Federal Response Plan[78] through the declaration of a State of Emergency. This declaration is based on the request of a governor, not unilateral decision making by the federal government. Once a declaration is in effect all of the resources of the federal government become available to assist the state. The process for providing such assistance is outlined in the Federal Response Plan, as is the responsibility of each participating federal department and agency. Assistance to the State is provided through a Federal Coordinating Officer who receives requests from state and local officials and ensures federal assets are provided as required. The Federal Response Plan includes a terrorism annex that discusses the difference between crisis and consequence management and the responsibilities assigned in PDD-39. The authority of the lead federal agency for the crisis resolution is derived from PDD-39, while the authority for the consequences management is derived from the Stafford Act. In both cases the Presidential Directive provides guidance to executive departments but only in the case of the disaster recovery is there statutory authority. As a result, when the law enforcement community led by the FBI manages the crisis phase of the operation it is not required to do so in support of the state, unlike FEMA who operates in support of the state.

Unlike Lopez, which demonstrated that federal usurpation of authority regarding public safety would not withstand public or judicial scrutiny, the Stafford Act and the National Response Plan have proven to be in harmony with the Constitution and the separation of powers. Since 1976 there has been 861 Major Disaster Declarations[79] and federal responses without a court challenge to the appropriateness of federal involvement in public safety. The difference is how the federal role was applied, in a preemptive manner or in a supporting role. The Lopez case highlights the limits of the Congress to mandate federal law enforcement involvement in public safety issues. A response to terrorism in the United States will require federal involvement due to the complexity of the threat and unique national capabilities[80]. In order to ensure that national assets are utilized in a timely and coordinated fashion, Congress must provide the authorities under which the crisis phase of a terrorist operation would be conducted. Like the Stafford Act, this authority must provide for federal assistance and that assistance must be in support of the State, at the request of the Governor. Lacking appropriate legislation, the authorities for a national response will remain ambiguous and the ability to resolve a crisis prior to it becoming a disaster will not be improved. The actions of terrorist on September 11 have heightened the awareness of Americans and the President has issued new Executive Orders to address the current emergency. The direction of the President is sound and like Lincoln and Roosevelt his application of Executive Powers to combat an emergency is prudent. However, in the case of combating terrorism, presidential directives have not been followed up with effective legislation. As a result, the federal government is not prepared to protect Americans during the crisis phase of a terrorist act. The lack of legislation has allowed the agencies within the executive branch to operate in an uncoordinated fashion and prevented appropriate Congressional oversight. As an example, in a GAO Audit titled Issues to be Resolved to Improve Counterterrorism Operations the following observation was made: "In reviewing DOD's participation in domestic support operations, special events and exercises, we found several command and control issues where guidance was either confusing or conflicting."[81]

4

The Need for New Legislation

Although there is an important distinction between a natural disaster and an act of terrorism the national regulation of each should acknowledge that the States have the primary responsibility for dealing with both. The role of the national government in both cases is to assist the State.

Disaster Assistance

The Disaster Relief Act of 1974, later known as the Robert B. Stafford Act, was signed into law on 22 May 1974.[82] This legislation has been amended only twice in nearly thirty years and has never been challenged in the Supreme Court despite its broad application.

Unlike Lopez, which directed federal officials to assume responsibility for protecting public safety, the Stafford Act directs the federal government to assist the states. As mentioned earlier, the Stafford Act is focused on the response to a disaster, not the actions that might be taken to prevent a disaster from occurring. The Stafford Act has been used to respond to hurricanes, ice storms, floods and other natural disasters.

As in the response to the consequences of a catastrophic event led by FEMA, in support of the states, the federal response to interdict or prevent a terrorist act should be led by a federal agency in support of the state. Natural disasters, unlike acts of terrorism, are events that are assumed to be outside the ability of man to influence. Acts of terrorism are intentional acts and therefore can be prevented. If they are to be effective the application of preventive measures must be made in a manner that is rapid and well coordinated. Terrorists are not required to follow a set pattern or attack a specific target. They are not restricted to any type of attack or technique. The result of the broad scope of the terrorist threat is that the United States must be prepared to protect its citizens anywhere, at any time and against whatever threat the terrorist might choose to employ. Local law enforcement has the ability to effectively deal with a terrorist act that is limited in scope and does not require specialty skills such as the dismantlement of a terrorist constructed nuclear device. The role of the federal government in preventing acts of terrorism must compliment the capabilities of the local and state officials, not replace them.

This chapter will review the Stafford Act and provide the information necessary to craft legislation that would allow for the use of special national teams under the leadership of the FBI while preserving for the states the ability to exercise police powers and preserve the health and safety of its citizens.

Unique Federal Capabilities

The success of the Stafford Act is based on the application of national response teams and capabilities to assist states when the scope of the disaster exceeds the ability of the state to respond. In the case of terrorism, the federal government has a broad array of capabilities that would be too expensive or simply impractical to duplicate on a local level or even state level. There are approximately nineteen thousand[83] police departments in the United States. The spending on one national response team at the FBI to maintain a Hostage Rescue Team's Weapons of Mass Destruction Program[84] is three and one half million dollars per year. The cost of duplicating this single capability in each police department would cost almost seventy billion dollars each year. The overall FBI counterterrorism budget for the same year was approximately one hundred million dollars, thirty times the costs of one program.

The weapon of mass destruction function within the FBI's Hostage Rescue Team is only a small part of only one agency's capabilities. Within the federal government there are five major agencies that maintain twenty-five separate response teams that all to provide some special expertise to help prevent terrorist acts involving weapons of mass destruction.[85] Since the federal government has the ability to draw on specialized experts from various agencies to provide assistance the level of education and experience of national teams exceeds that available to local and state police officers. Only fourteen percent of all local law enforcement officers in the United States have some college education, contrasted with the FBI's requirement that all entry-level agents have a minimum of a bachelor degree.[86] The federal government's Centers for Disease Control is staffed with experts in all forms of health hazards including deadly bio-toxins such as anthrax. It would be impracticable to maintain cadres of highly trained experts employed at the local level to perform such specialized tasks. The education, experience and technological assets of the federal government must be made available to states in order for the states to carry out their responsibility to protect the public.

New legislation to provide such assistance the Congress must adequately define the scope of the assistance in clear and unambiguous language. The first step in the process is including in the legislation definitions that will ensure all those involved in an activity are operating with a common understanding of objectives.

Conflicting Mandates

Current legislation makes it very difficult to identify what roles and responsibilities of the federal agencies are because definitions are missing from some legislation and conflicting in others. One example is the lack of a clear, concise and consistent definition of weapons of mass destruction.

The definition of "weapon of mass destruction" is not included in the US Code on terrorism.[87] 18 USC 842 (p)(1)(c) includes the language "weapon of mass destruction has the same meaning as in section 2332a(c)(2)." Section 2332 states: "the term weapon of mass destruction means—any destructive device as defined in section 921 of this title; any weapon that is designed or intended to cause death or serious bodily injury through the release, dissemination, or impact of toxic or poisonous chemicals, or their precursors; any weapon involving a disease organism; or any weapon that is designed to release radiation or radioactivity at a level dangerous to human life." Section 921 of Title 18 provides list of items that are considered to be destructive and thereby qualify to be considered weapons of mass destruction.

At the end of this search for a definition of "weapon of mass destruction" one can conclude that almost anything that can cause harm to a person meets the criteria set out in federal law. The continuing expansion of the definition of a "weapon of mass destruction" has in part led to the ever-expanding role of national response teams.

Without Congressional mandates to provide assistance, executive agencies such as the FBI have used the criminal prosecution powers of Title 18 violations as the authority to claim jurisdiction over all terrorist activity. The net effect of this ambiguity in definitions is that one cannot determine where the state and local authorities end and where the national response authorities step in. Nearly every conceivable act that could result in injury is subject to a federal claim of jurisdiction without due deference to the state.

Once the definitions of what the legislation addresses are made clear and unambiguous there must be a determination of what the federal government will provide in the way of assistance in the prevention phase of a terrorist event. Using the model of the Stafford Act, this begins with an outline of preparedness activities. In the case of terrorism, preparedness activities mandated by the Congress and undertaken by the Executive have focused primarily on recovery and response, not prevention. The Defense Against Weapons of Mass Destruction Act of 1996 directed the president to undertake to "enhance the Federal capability to prevent and respond to terrorist incidents involving WMDs; and support State and local efforts to improve their response to such incidents.[88]" The definition of "weapon of mass destruction" was somewhat refined as part of this Act to "means any weapon or device that is intended, or has the capability, to cause death or serious bodily injury to a significant number of people through the release, dissemination, or impact of—(A) toxic or poisonous chemicals or their precursors; (B) a disease organism; or (C) radiation or radioactivity." Of note is that the legislation does not change the Title 18 authorities under which the FBI operates; it merely limits the responsibility of the Defense Department to provide assistance to a more specific range of activities. This difference in definition creates confusion as to what federal assets are authorized for use to prevent a disaster and under what circumstances. While the Act does direct the President to assist state and local government officials to prevent acts of terrorism it does not specify how nor does the Act provide any measures to assess the effectiveness of the assistance.

Another piece of legislation that sounds like it would address the issue of preventing acts of terror was introduced into the Senate as the Comprehensive Terrorism Prevention Act of 1995. When the Act was signed into law its name had changed to the Anti-terrorism and Effective Death Penalty Act of 1996. The name change probably reflects the realization that the Act would do nothing to prevent terrorism. There is nothing in the Act that specifically addresses actions to be taken to actually stop a terrorist act that is underway. Habeas Corpus Reform, Justice for Victims, Terrorist and Criminal Alien Removal and Exclusion, Nuclear Biological and Chemical Weapons Restrictions and Criminal Law Modifications to Counter Terrorism are of the major sections of the Act. The Act expands the authorities under which the federal government can prosecute, but that methodology requires a crime be committed. In effect, for the law to have any impact it requires acts of terrorism be carried out.

While the tradition of American justice has been to use penalties such as the death penalty as a deterrent, that will not be effective in an environment where the terrorist plans suicide as part of the crime. Actions must focus on stopping the terrorist prior to achieving his or her goal, not prosecuting them after the fact.

The Congress should use the definition of weapons of mass destruction found in the Defense Against Weapons of Mass Destruction Act of 1996 as a starting point for determining what the federal government should be prepared to provide to states.

The federal government has numerous specialized teams that claim expertise in protecting citizens from chemical or biological agents as well as radiological materials. The Army Technical Escort Unit[89] and the FBI Hazardous Material Response Unit[90] both advertise similar capabilities with a significant difference being that the Army does not use the words "criminal activity" while the FBI description of capabilities specifies that its capabilities are used to responds to criminal acts.

It is significant to note neither organization's web site discussing their capabilities includes language to indicate the capabilities could be used to protect the public. The Department of Defense, wary of criticism for treading into areas of law enforcement because of legislative restrictions has not viewed domestic response as a primary mission. While this view may be changing as a result of the September 11 terrorist attacks, it is rooted in core beliefs dating back to the colonial period that the military should not be used in the enforcement of laws within the United States.[91] The FBI description of its capability specifies the response to a crime as the objective, not the protection of Americans. New legislation must make it clear that the capabilities resident in the federal system are to protect citizens as their primary function.

A State-Federal Team

Expert advice and technical support to ensure state and local officials have the same knowledge about whether terrorist act is likely, being planned or already underway is a critical component of a national response plan. Current legislation does not direct the Executive to notify a Governor if a terrorist act is imminent or already underway. Additionally, there is nothing in current legislation that requires the federal authorities to inform a state that a national response may be underway, thus removing the ability of state officials to weigh the impact on public safety of such actions. New legislation must include specific actions that federal agencies will take and the federal agencies must address what official is authorized to direct those actions. The new legislation must also include provisions that require the federal government to share information with state officials regarding terrorism threats and responses. To accomplish this the federal government should insure that key personnel in each state are granted national level security clearances that will allow them to receive classified briefings about terrorist threats and classified national response plans. Defining the specific role of the federal government in providing information and assistance will ensure that state officials are eligible to receive the information required to make informed request for assistance.

Once what the federal government will provide at the request of the states is determined, how that assistance is provided must be directed through legislation. In order to avoid interagency competition for control, there must be statutory authority for the federal incident manager to effectively coordinate and direct a response. Since the response to prevent a terrorist act is likely to be time critical the assignment of the management responsibility must be clear and unambiguous and must be a standing authority. Within the FBI there is a Critical Incident Response Group that was specifically created to manage complex incidents that require federal assistance during a crisis. The Critical Incident Response Group mission statement reads: "The Critical Incident Response Group (CIRG) facilitates the FBI's rapid response to, and the management of, crisis incidents. CIRG was established in 1994 to integrate tactical and investigative resources and expertise for critical incidents that necessitate an immediate response from law enforcement authorities. CIRG will deploy investigative specialists to respond to terrorist activities, hostage takings, child abductions and other high-risk repetitive violent crimes. Other major incidents include prison riots, bombings, air and train crashes, and natural disasters."[92] A core component of the Critical Incident Response Group is the Hostage Rescue Team. The Hostage Rescue Team is an FBI capability specifically designed to protect citizens, in fact the motto of the Hostage Rescue Team is "servare vitas" in english "To Save Lives."[93] Congress assigning the responsibility to manage an incident is not without precedent. The Goldwater-Nichols Department of Defense Reorganization Act of 1986 required the Department of Defense to establish a new chain of command for the commanders of each military region, known as Combatant Commanders. The Act required that operational flow of information and decision-making go directly from the Combatant Commander to the President and Secretary of Defense, bypassing the Pentagon Bureaucracy.[94]

Like the complex military structure that still exists the law enforcement organizations within the United States are large and often not well coordinated. A General Accounting Office Audit of counterterrorism activities noted "Based on our analysis of the [Bureau of Alcohol Tobacco and Firearms'][95] program, it appears ATF is exercising its lead in incidents in which the FBI, not ATF should lead. The lack of coordination on [field training]exercises between these two law enforcement agencies could reduce the effectiveness of the total federal response to a terrorist incident and lead to duplication of effort."[96]

Interagency and internal agency turf battles are not uncommon. The gravity of the situation when attempting to prevent an act of terrorism requires a clear legislative mandate for one federal government office to effectively manage the federal response. The FBI has created a Critical Incident Response Group that has the ability to manage complex operations over a broad range of threats and in hostile or non-hostile environments. Congress should provide the necessary authorities for the Critical Incident Response Group Commander to manage such incidents just as it did for the military commanders in Goldwater-Nichols.

Having discussed what should be provided to states and who should control the response the next requirement of effective legislation will be to define the methodology for activating the support. The Stafford Act provides an excellent model of the request process that would need only minor modifications to be effective for preventing terrorism. The procedure for activating federal assistance under the Stafford Act is as follows. A Governor must make a request to the President for a declaration that a major disaster exists. He must specify that the severity of the disaster exceeds the ability of the state to protect life. He must also provide specific information about the scope of the emergency, exactly what state and local assets are overwhelmed and require assistance and agree to cost-sharing arrangements.

While all of that data is relevant in once a disaster has occurred, one must ask how a Governor would provide the information required to seek federal assistance to prevent a man made disaster if it has not yet occurred. Since the Stafford Act was based on providing assistance primarily to recover from natural disasters it does not detail procedures that one would follow to prevent the disaster.

There are several ways in which an incident might be anticipated: (1) an overt threat; (2) intelligence collection; (3) law enforcement activities. In any of those cases the Governor will not have the result of a disaster to assess, rather the possibility of one occurring. This poses a new set of problems for intergovernmental relationships that will need to be addressed in the legislation.

In the case of an overt threat, one could assume that a notification of an imminent threat is provided. The Irish Republican Army uses coded threat warnings to the British authorities when it plants a bomb, allowing the authorities to evacuate the area but not providing enough time to disarm the bomb. In this case the motive is publicity, not loss of human life. The British method of managing these incidents is very well practiced, but it is practiced using a national system of law enforcement, not one that includes multiple levels of government with distributed authorities.

In the United States, if a terrorist threat came into a governmental office or through the media it is not clear that state officials would know exactly how to request assistance or what to ask for. If the information was obtained by the one of the fifty-six FBI field division offices spread out throughout the country, the FBI Special Agent in Charge would be in position to brief state officials on the scope of the threat, the possible effects of the threat being proven accurate, what federal assets could be used to mitigate the threat and what the risk is to the general public.

This information would allow the Governor to request federal assistance based on probably results of the disaster, not actual results. By requiring the FBI to provide support to the state in the request process, the legislation would ensure critical communications between local FBI personnel who know the area and national teams lead by FBI officials begin as soon as a threat becomes known. The Governor would then submit a request to the President based on all available information and the President would issue a declaration of imminent disaster.

The collection of intelligence abroad might tell us of the possibility of an act of terrorism. This offers a new set of considerations since the national intelligence community would not normally provide classified briefings to the Governor of a state. In recent Congressional testimony, Robert Mueller, Director of the FBI, stated that the policy of the FBI is to share any specific threat information with State authorities. Given the current political and security environments it is reasonable to assume that there would be almost unlimited sharing of information, and the President's leadership in a time of emergency would guarantee the sharing of threat information. That being said, the emergency will likely fade, as did the nullification crisis, the great depression and even Clinton's state of emergency on the proliferation of weapons of mass destruction. When the emergency does begin to fade and the current drive to handle terrorism as the top national security priority fades with it there must be legislation that removes the personal leadership factor from the equation. President Bush, the Director of Homeland Security Governor Ridge, Director Mueller are doing exceptional jobs at protecting Americans in a time of emergency, the Congress now needs to ensure that protection lasts into the future and is codified in appropriate federal law. The last chapter of this thesis will provide a draft bill that could serve as the basis for new legislation.

5

A Proposed Bill

Presidents have the ability to wield exceptional authority to manage crises and the Congress has the responsibility to follow up with legislation that allows the continuation of Presidential actions or directs those action cease. The preceding chapters have outlined the development of a system of governing that is outside the constitutional framework established by the Founders.

Development of Policy in Secret

The federal government's management of national security activities is not carried on with the consent of the governed, but is without the knowledge of the governed. Emergency Presidential authorities are not new. President Jackson used them during the Nullification Crisis, President Lincoln during the Civil War and President Franklin during the Depression. Recent Presidents have used the power of executive during emergencies to deal with crises but in the case of preventing terrorism Congress has not fulfilled its responsibility to follow up with legislation.

The use of executive powers to expand the role of federal government without Congressional sanction has led to a national counterterrorism program that is uncoordinated, redundant and less effective that it should be. This is the result of the process the recent administrations have used to direct counterterrorism activities. Presidents since Richard Nixon have not sought enabling legislation from the Congress for counterterrorism programs. Nor have they used Executive Orders that are published in the Federal Register and subject to public scrutiny and debate. Instead, counterterrorism policies have been directed through a series of National Security Directives that are normally classified, limited in distribution and rarely publicly debated.[97]

The use of National Security Directives to direct actions by the executive agencies is an appropriate method for the President to act quickly to protect the

United States. When the President declares a state of emergency, or simply believes there is a danger to the security of the nation, actions are required that cannot wait upon the deliberative processes of the Congress. Like all chief executives, Presidents must be able to act when the situation calls for action. The Commander-in-Chief clause of the Constitution gives the President the powers necessary to use the resources of the federal government in a timely manner. The Constitution does not extend that authority to the development of long-term government programs, which is reserved to the Congress.

The Case for Congressional Action

The Congress is accountable to the people to define the actions that should be undertaken by the Executive and provide funding and oversight for the actions of the executive branch. In the case of preventing terrorism, Congress has not fulfilled this responsibility. There have been presidential directives on terrorism since the Nixon Administration reacted to the massacre at the Munich Olympics in 1972. Billions of tax dollars have been spent on terrorism-related programs during this period. However, in every instance Congress has failed to codify the responsibilities of the federal government in supporting efforts to prevent terrorism within the states.

Federal support to the States to protect citizens from acts of terror remains less than adequate because the Congress has not yet defined the role of the federal government. Federal agencies have been left on their own to define authority, strategy and mission. The General Accounting Office has provided a series of reports that give ample information upon which to act. Presidents have fulfilled their responsibility to take emergency actions, and done so quite effectively. The obligation of the legislative branch to review Presidential directives on counterterrorism is clear.

It is foolish to think that acts of terror will not be attempted again in the United States. Global conflict has widened for decades and the weapon of choice is terrorism. Americans must be protected from acts of terror. Prevention is the only true method. Planning for response and recovery after an attack is necessary but it is a recipe for disaster if it is our sole policy.

The following draft bill is model legislation that would force better coordination among federal agencies. The bill defines and assigns roles, responsibilities and accountability within the federal government. It also mandates that the federal government take act to stop or prevent terrorist acts in support of the states, consistent with the Constitution.

Most important in the bill is the requirement for the federal agencies to share information with the states and involve the states in planning to prevent terrorism. Only by working together will the various levels and branches of government be able to prevent additional acts of terror in the United States.

A Bill

Entitled the "Prevention of Domestic Terrorism Assistance Act of 2002"

TITLE I—FINDINGS, DECLARATIONS, AND DEFINITIONS

FINDINGS AND DECLARATIONS

Sec.101 (a) The Congress hereby finds and declares that—

1. Because the threat of terrorist activity within the United States is a threat to the national security, the national economy and the preservation of civil freedom of the citizens; and

2. because terrorist activity committed in the United States is a criminal act punishable by state and federal statutes; and

3. because the Constitution reserves to the States the responsibility to protect the public from criminal activity through the use of police powers; and

4. because the federal government has at its disposal national and unique response capabilities that if applied correctly could prevent a successful terrorist attack from taking place within the United States; and

5. because these unique national capabilities cannot be duplicated within the States because of fiscal constraints and a limited pool of expertise;

(b) It is the intent of the Congress to provide an orderly and continuing means of assistance by the Federal Government to State governments in carrying out their responsibilities to protect the public from acts of terrorism which exceed the capabilities of local and State officials by—

1. developing protocols by which intelligence obtained by the federal government that a terrorist attack is either threatened or imminent be immediately shared with the Governor and key security personnel of the affected State;

2. revising all federal and national terrorism response plans to include language that requires immediate notification of a threat to the affected State's Security Officials; and

3. coordinating with the affected State leadership in the development of response plans and procedures prior to the deployment of national assets into a State; and

4. directing that all national response capabilities available to the federal government be made available to the Governor of a state upon request by the State; and

5. implementing a training and readiness program that requires routine exercising of national response plans with State and local participation.

DEFINITIONS[98]

Sec. 102. As used in this Act—

1. "Terrorism" means any criminal act that has the intent of causing loss of life or property through violence to further a political objective.

2. "National Response Capability" means any federal funded program or team of personnel which reside in a federal agency that have capabilities to track, identify, interdict, interrupt, mitigate, or prevent acts of terrorism. Any federal program that receives funding from the Congress for anti-terrorism, counterterrorism, or weapons of mass destruction activities is subject to this Act.

3. "Intelligence" means any information collected by federal agencies through overt or covert activities that provides information as to the intent or capabilities of terrorists, terrorist groups or state sponsors of terrorism.

4. "Weapon of Mass Destruction" means any device that contains nuclear or radiological materials, biological materials, or chemical agents or chemical agent precursors that is constructed to release said materials in a fashion that would or could cause harm to the public, or any component of such device; and any part of the national infrastructure, such as but not limited to aircraft, vehicles, trains, electric generation facilities, and dams during such time that those components of the infrastructure are used as the means to cause destruction or injury.

5. "State" means the fifty States, the District of Columbia, Puerto Rico, the Virgin Islands, Guam, American Samoa and the Trust Territory of the Pacific Islands.

6. "State Security Officials" means the Governor, Lieutenant Governor, State Adjutant General, Chief of the State Police, Sate Attorney General and the Director of the State Office of Homeland Security and the appropriate leadership in the state legislatures

7. "Federal Agency" means any department, independent establishment, Government corporation, or other agency of the executive branch of the Federal Government, including the United States Postal Service.

TITLE II—Terrorism Prevention Assistance

FEDERAL AND STATE INFORMATION SHARING PROGRAMS

Sec. 201. (a) The President is authorized to establish a program for the sharing of intelligence and technical information relating to terrorists, terrorism and terrorism programs between States and federal agencies. The President shall use the services of all appropriate agencies, under the leadership of the Federal Bureau of Investigation to ensure:

1. State Security Officials in each state are granted TOP SECRET national security clearances to allow for the sharing of intelligence and threat information; and

2. each FBI Field Division will provide classified material storage and briefing facilities for the utilization of State Security Officials; and

3. the Director of the FBI will require each Field Division Special Agent in Charge to notify the State any time intelligence indicates a specific threat of terrorism exists that targets a specific State; and

4. each federal agency that has national response capabilities will conduct an annual briefing for State Security Officials on such capabilities and include in those briefings the following:

   a. the specific capabilities of the national response capability and how the capabilities differ from those available within the state;

   b. the location and response time (to the State) of the capability; and

   c. past interaction between the national response teams and State agencies has taken place; and

> d. procedures for requesting national assistance and the process by which decisions are made the federal level to commit national assets.

5. Statement of applicability. Each terrorism related intelligence briefing to the President or heads of federal agencies shall include a statement as to whether the intelligence is applicable to the States. If the statement of applicability indicates that there is reason to brief the states the President shall direct, or the agency head shall request, that the Director of the FBI arrange such a briefing.

(b) The President will, through the Director of the FBI, report to Congress annually the number of terrorist threats identified and the action taken to in each case to share threat information with the States.

NATIONAL CONTINGENCY PLAN FOR THE PREVENTION OF TERRORIST ACTS

Sec. 202. (a) The President shall direct that existing National Response Plans be modified to include the requirement that all national response assets deployed into a state to combat terrorism be deployed at the request of the Governor.

(b) The Director of the FBI will establish a task force chaired by the Executive Assistant Director for Counterterrorism and consisting of representatives of each agency funded to provide a terrorism response capability to review all current terrorism response plans and develop a "National Contingency Plan for the Prevention of Terrorist Acts" within 180 days of this Act becoming law. The National Contingency Plan for the Prevention of Terrorist Acts will include:

1. Identification of national response capabilities. Each federal agency that has terrorism response capabilities will be identified in the Plan and the capabilities of that agency will be described as to how that capability can be used to stop acts of terrorism within the United States.

2. Assignment of incident command relationships.

3. Procedures for the deployment of national response capabilities to the States

TERRORISM PREVENTION EMERGENCY SUPPORT TEAMS

Sec. 203 (a) The President shall, in each case of a domestic terrorism prevention deployment dispatch a team consisting of representatives of federal agencies with national response assets. A Senior Member of the FBI Critical Incident Response Group will lead the Terrorism Prevention Emergency Support Team and upon the request of the President, each agency Head will detail personnel to the team for the duration of the deployment. The Team will:

(b) provide advice to State Security Officials on the specific threat and the likelihood of success by the terrorists; what national response capabilities can be brought to bear to prevent the attack from taking place; and what federal assets are available to mitigate the effects of the potential attack; and

(c) provide advice to State Security Officials as to the potential scope of an incident to include the consequences of the attack succeeding in potential loss of life, destruction of property; and

(d) act as a liaison between federal agencies and State Security Officials throughout the incident, provide the necessary communications hardware and expertise to ensure that lines of communication are established and maintained between the Governor and the White House, national response teams and State Security Officials; the FBI Critical Incident Response Commander and the Governor; and

(e) Assist the State Security Officials with the development of a request to the President for national response capability deployment to resolve the incident.

PROCEDURES FOR REQUESTING FEDERAL ASSISTANCE

Sec 204. (a) The President is authorized to provide assistance to a State for the purpose of preventing a terrorist attack upon receipt of a written request from the Governor for a of the affected state under the following conditions:

1. The Governor has received a briefing that the likelihood exists that a terrorist attack will take place within the State involving the use of a Weapon of Mass Destruction; and

2. The request includes the specific national response capabilities that are required and defined the limits of the Governor to resolve the incident without the assistance of national response capabilities; and

3. The request is limited to federal assistance for potential terrorist acts involving weapons of mass destruction as defined in Section 102; or

4. The potential terrorist attack involves terrorist tactics or capabilities that exceed the ability of local and state law enforcement to prevent; or

5. Multiple attacks are suspected, thereby requiring a response that exceeds the capability of the State to respond to all incident sites.

    a. In the case of multiple incidents the Incident Commander, as designated by the Governor, will exercise operational control over national response assets.

(b) Upon determining that a request for assistance meets the requirements of part (a), the President shall declare that a State of Emergency exists due to imminent terrorist attack and will direct the FBI to activate national response teams under the command and control of the Commander, FBI Critical Incident Response Group, designated the National Terrorism Prevention Response Commander.

1. Within four hours of the receipt of a request for a declaration of a state of emergency, a Terrorism Prevention Emergency Support Team will be dispatched to perform the responsibilities described in section 203 of the Bill.

2. Upon request of the National Terrorism Prevention Response Commander, all federal agencies will make available national response capabilities described in the National Terrorism Prevention Contingency Plan for deployment to the affected State under the command and control of the National Terrorism Prevention Response Commander.

3. The Department of Defense will provide airlift support to transport the Terrorism Prevention Emergency Support Team to the requesting State for coordination with the Governor and to move national response assets at the direction of the National Terrorism Prevention Response Commander.

RESPONSE PLAN INTEGRATION

Section 205 (a) The President shall establish a program to assist States in developing terrorism prevention contingency plans that—

1. define the capabilities of the state to detect and prevent terrorist acts through the use of information sharing, preventative police work, community involvement and awareness and active response to interdict or disrupt activities underway; and

2. that outline how the State will organize to conduct terrorism prevention operations; and

3. defines the State decision making authorities and procedures for requesting federal assistance.

(b) The State Terrorism Prevention Contingency Plans will be developed to ensure that once there is a decision by the State that a potential terrorist attack could exceed the capabilities of the State there is a procedure in place to accept national response assets into the State's Incident Command System.

(c) The Director of the FBI will submit to the Congress each year a report that identifies which states participate in this program and a statement as to whether each state's Plan is integrated into the national plan.

TRAINING AND READINESS PROGRAM

Section 206 (a) The President shall establish a program to assist the states in becoming less dependent on the federal government to prevent acts of terrorism through an aggressive training and readiness program that includes—

1. Development of a methodology for assessing the readiness of each police force to prevent acts of terrorism through an understanding of terrorist capabilities and an analysis of capabilities of local and state officials to respond to non-weapons of mass destruction incidents;

2. Training for local and state terrorist prevention response teams on all aspects of terrorist interdiction other than when dealing with weapons of mass destruction. Weapons of mass destruction training for state and local responders will be provided at the request of the Governor only if the State has demonstrated through joint exercises that it has the capa-

bility to prevent non-weapons of mass destruction terrorist attacks and the state is committed to expend the additional resources required to train and maintain specialized teams to prevent nuclear, chemical or biological attacks.

3. Training for law enforcement in the detection and identification of materials used to develop weapons of mass destruction, personal protective measures and immediate actions required to protect the public; and

4. Training for incident commanders on national response capabilities and national terrorism prevention contingency plans and the integration of local, state and federal assets during an incident; and

5. Conducting terrorism prevention exercises with each State annually. The exercises conducted will be coordinated by the FBI Field Division SAC and will be conducted utilizing a three year cycle that includes—

    a. table top exercises designed to revalidate response plans and asset integration; and

    b. command post exercises designed to validate communications and decision making processes; and

    c. field training exercises designed to practice all aspects of a terrorism prevention response.

(b). The Director of the FBI will report to the Congress each year on the status of the training and readiness program which will include an assessment of the readiness of state and local agencies to prevent acts of terror and detail lessons learned in the exercise program that require federal resources to correct.

Title III—Criminal Prosecution

Sec 301 (a) The President is authorized to seek federal prosecution of terrorist apprehended during the planning or the attempt to conduct an act of terrorism only when such prosecution does not interfere with the State's responsibility to protect the public. In all cases, the prevention of a terrorist act will take precedence over the development of a prosecutorial chain of evidence or the withholding of sensitive information that, while may assist in prosecution, would detract from preventing the terrorist act.

(b) This Act does not change any of the current law regarding prosecution and punishment of terrorist. Criminal prosecution of terrorists should be conducted vigorously utilizing current statutes as long as the investigation does not interfere with the prevention of a terrorist act.

Endnotes

1. Alexis De Tocqueville, *Democracy in America*, J. P Mayer Ed., trans. George Lawrence (New York: Harper and Row, 1969), 114.

2. Clinton Rossiter, Ed., *The Federalist Papers* (New York: The Penguin Group, 1961), 292

3. *American Schools Directory,* 22 Nov. 2001, <http://www.asd.com/>

4. *Fairfax County Public School System Operating Budget for FY2001 Page,* 3 Oct. 2001, <http://www.fcps.edu>

5. *The Impact Aid Act. Statutes at Large* 108, sec. 3844, (1994)

6. *The Individuals with Disabilities Act. Statutes at Large,* 89, sec.733 (1975)

7. *United States v. Lopez,* 514 U.S. 549 (1995)

8. Rossiter, 410

9. *Los Angeles Times* (Los Angeles), 4 August 1980. Eric Lichtblau details an of appointment by President Clinton in which he used the recess appointment clause of the Constitution to bypass the Senate confirmation process. Bill Lann Lee, a Clinton appointee to the Justice Department was not confirmed by the Senate which never had an up or down vote on Mr. Lee. Mr. Lee did serve in the Justice Position until the end of the Clinton Administration but was never confirmed by the Senate.

10. The term "federal" during the period that the government was being formed was closer to our current definition of a confederacy than to our current understanding of a federal system.

11. Rossiter, 243–246

12. By using the term "delegated" in the text of the Constitution the Framers make it abundantly clear that the scope of federal authority is determined by the states, not the federal government itself.

13. In all discussions in this thesis regarding Madison's Notes I use 1987 printing by W.W. Norton and Company.

14. James Madison, *Notes of the Debates in the Federal Convention of 1787*, with an introduction by Adrienne Koch (New York: W.W. Norton and Company, 1987), 29

15. Madison, 153. Discussion between Mr. King and Mr. Wilson during the debate on Tues, June 19, 1787 regarding which authorities would rest in a federal government and the status of the individual states.

16. Madison, 78–79

17. Leonard Levy, *Original Intent and the Framers' Constitution* (New York: Macmillan, 1988), 38

18. Rossiter, 396. In Federalist 64, Jay discusses the method of appointment of Senators by the State legislatures and the impact that they would have on the ratification process associated with treaties.

19. *Gibbons v. Ogden*, 22 U.S. 1 (1824)

20. Frederic Bancroft, *Calhoun and the South Carolina Nullification Movement* (Gloucester: Peter Smith 1966), 3. From a speech from John C. Calhoun in Congress, April 4, 1816 in support of the tariff bill.

21. Bancroft, 6–8

22. Bancroft, 19–22

23. Bancroft, 129

24. Chauncey Samuel Boucher, *The Nullification Controversy in South Carolina* (New York: Greenwood Press, 1968), 285–289

25. Dean Sprague, *Freedom Under Lincoln* (Boston: Houghton Mifflin, 1965), 116–117.

26. *Ex Parte Merryman*, (1861)

27. Sprague, 118

28. Sprague, 203

29. Sprague, 142–151

30. Paul Craig Roberts and Lawrence M. Stratton, "The Fed's Depression and the Birth of the New Deal," *Policy Review*, no. 108 (2001) 20

31. *The Federal Reserve Act of 1913, Statues at Large*, 6 sec. 32 (1913)

32. Roberts and Stratton, 27

33. This will also be addressed in more detail in a following section on the use of Presidential declarations and orders to justify requesting new authorities or funds from Congress.

34. *National Archives and Records Administration Web Site,* 15 January 2002, The number and title of each executive order since 1929 is provided by the National Archives along with a description of the role of the Executive Order in governing. <http://www.nara.gov/fedreg/eo.html#top>

35. *Executive Order 12954,* (1995)

36. There is a legitimate concern for security of the information contained in many the National Security documents that must protected from public discloser.

37. President Kennedy issued National Security Action Memorandum 50 (NSAM-50) to address the launching into space systems involving nuclear power.

38. Joseph Shattan, *Architects of Victory, Six Heroes of the Cold War* (Washington: The Heritage Foundation, 1999), 4–5. Ronald Reagan issued National Security Decision Directive 75 (NSDD-75). The document was recently declassified and outlines his approach to ensuring the economic collapse of the Soviet Union. The Reagan administration followed this strategy that helped bring about the eventual demise of the Soviet Union.

39. C.H Hoebeke, *The Road to Mass Democracy* (New Brunswick: Transaction Publishers, 1995), 19–20

40. Hedrick Smith, *The Power Game* (New York: Ballantine Books, 1988) 20–21

41. Smith, 24–25

42. Smith, 29

43. First Responders include firefighters, police, and emergency medical personnel that would normal be among the first to respond to an incident or accident.

44. *Defense Against Weapons of Mass Destruction Act of 1996,* Statutes at Large 110 Sec. 2714 (1996)

45. Rossiter, 465

46. Paul Craig Roberts, and Lawrence M Stratton, *The New Color Line* (Washington: Regnery Publishing, 1995) 34–35

47. *Spallone v. United States,* 107 L Ed 2d

48. On 11 September four hijacked airliners were used to attack the World Trade Center twin towers in New York City and the Pentagon in Arlington, VA. The death toll of the combined attacks approaches 5,000; double the death toll of the Pearl Harbor attack in December 1941.

49. Rossiter, 38–39

50. Rossiter, 172–174

51. Peter S. Onuf, Ed., *Jeffersonian Legacies,* (Charlottesville: University of Virginia Press, 1993) 378

52. By the act creating the War Department, August 7, 1789 (1 Stat. 49).

53. *Veterans of Foreign Wars Web Site,* 25 Feb. 2002, <http://www.vfw.org/member/elig2.shtml>The VFW web site provides a list of military campaigns in which American service members participated. The VFW list includes 101 campaigns since 1874 alone, this does not include the Indian Wars, the Mexican American War, the War of 1812 and other smaller campaigns.

54. *History of the FBI Web Page,* 25 Feb. 2002 <http://www.fbi.gov/fbinbrief/historic/history>

55. *18 US Code Section 2151* To be categorized as an act of sabotage the act must be one that injures national defense or warfighting capabilities through the destruction of facilities or materials.

56. Title 18 US Code provides the statutory authorities for FBI investigation of crimes. The Title is broken down by category of crime and the FBI derives its authority to investigate from each individual section.

57. *History of the FBI Web Page,* 25 Feb. 2002. <http://www.fbi.gov/fbinbrief/historic/history>

58. Igor Beliaev and John Marks, Ed., *Common Ground on Terrorism, Soviet-American Cooperation Against the Politics of Terror* (New York: W.W.Norton and Co., 1991) 15

59. James M. Smith and William C. Thomas, Ed., *The Terrorism Threat and U.S. Government Response: Operational and Organizational Factors,*

(Golden: USAF Institute for National Security Studies, 2001) < http://www.usafa.af.mil/inss/terrorism.htm>

60. Smith and Thomas, 12

61. President, National Security Decision Directive-30, *Managing Terrorist Incidents,* (1982)

62. Martha Crenshaw, *Terrorism in Context* (University Park: Penn State University, 1995), 7

63. Federal Register, Vol. 59 no. 220, (1994)

64. General Accounting Office, *Combating Terrorism GAO/NSIAD-97–254,* (Washington, D.C.: GPO, 1997), 39–43. The difference between crisis and consequence management in is described in detailed in this GAO report. In summary, the FBI has the responsibility to detect and prevent acts of terror, to include stopping a terrorist in the process of attempting to commit the act. It is the management of that response to an event in progress that is categorized as crisis management. Activities such as a bomb blast or a plane crashing into a building move the management to a recovery phase, or consequences management, those efforts are lead by FEMA.

65. General Accounting Office, *Combating Terrorism GAO/NSIAD-97-254,* (Washington, D.C.: GPO, 1997), 73–78. In a series of audits on US Government counterterrorism programs the GAO provided a summary of all legislation pertaining to terrorism back to 1961. All legislation dealing with terrorism through 1995 was focused on international operations and foreign trade.

66. General Accounting Office, *Combating Terrorism GAO/NSIAD-97-254,* (Washington, D.C.: GPO, 1997), 46.

67. National Counterterrorism policy defines the response to terrorism in two phases, crisis and consequences management. In the crisis phase the FBI is the lead federal agency (except in the case of an aircraft hijacking) and in the consequence phase FEMA leads the federal efforts to assist the states.

68. *United States v. Lopez,* 514 U.S. 549 (1995)

69. US Constitution Article VI reads in part "This Constitution, and the Laws of the United States which shall be made in Pursuance thereof; and

all Treaties made, or which shall be made, under that authority of the United States, shall be the supreme law of the land."

70. *United States v. Lopez,* 131 L Ed 2d, 632, a discussion of the District Court action in the Lopez case provides the rationale by which the District Court decided the Act was a valid use of Congressional Powers

71. *U.S. Code* 18 Sec. 922(q)

72. Rossiter, 264

73. The stability of the market and the role of the federal government in assuring that stability is a topic subject to debate. Economists such as Milton Freidman believe that the best case is no government involvement and that a free market is self-regulating. Since it is common practice within the Congress to regulate for economic stability one must assume for the purposes of this paper that drafting legislation to fight terrorism could be based on the economic impact of terror, not on its affect on public safety.

74. Defense Against Weapons of Mass Destruction Act of 1996, Statutes at Large 110 Sec. 2714 (1996)

75. *Defense Against Weapons of Mass Destruction Act of 1996,* Statutes at Large 110 Sec. 2714 (1996)

76. *U.S. Code* 42 Sec. 5191

77. Section 102 of the Act defines emergencies and disasters to include hurricanes, tornados and flooding. The authorities under this act were expanded to include responses to acts of terrorism.

78. Federal Emergency Management Agency, *Federal Response Plan 9230.1-PL* (Washington, D.C.: GPO, 1999)

79. *History of the Federal Emergency Management Agency Web Page,* 12 Mar. 2002, <www.fema.gov/about/history.htm>

80. General Accounting Office, *Combating Terrorism GAO/NSIAD-97-254,* (Washington, D.C.: GPO, 1997)

81. General Accounting Office, *Combating Terrorism GAO/NSIAD-97-254,* (Washington, D.C.: GPO, 1997)

82. *The Disaster Relief Act, Statutes at Large* 88, sec. 164, (1974)

83. *The International Association of Chiefs of Police web site,* 12 Mar. 2002, <http://www.theiacp.org/faq.htm>

84. GAO-GGD-99-7,FBI's Use of Federal Funds for Counterterrorism, 41, Provides a breakdown of spending within the FBI to maintain counterterrorism capabilities. The budget numbers used for this thesis reflect fiscal year 1999 authorizations as reported by the GAO. The budget line in question is $3.5M per year.

85. General Accounting Office, *Combating Terrorism GAO/NSIAD-97-254,* (Washington, D.C.: GPO, 1997), 79

86. *Federal Bureau of Investigation Web Site*, 20 Feb 2002, <http:/www.fbi.gov>

87. Title 18 Chapter 113B, the chapter on terrorism makes no mention of weapons of mass destruction.

88. Public Law 104–201, Title XIV authorizes the Secretary of Defense to assist the States in the development of local and state capabilities to respond to acts of terrorism. Specifically, the federal agencies are to help firefighters and emergency medical personnel to be able to protect themselves in an attack like the one that took place in the Tokyo subway in 1995. During that attack, many fire and rescue worker were overcome by the chemicals that had been released and they became casualties as well.

89. United States Army, *Technical Escort Unit Web Site,* 20 Feb. 2002, <http://teu.sbccom.army.mil/factsheet.htm> States: "The United States Army Technical Escort Unit provides the Department of Defense and other federal agencies with a unique, immediate response capability for chemical and biological warfare material. The Tech Escort missions include worldwide response for escorting, packaging, detection, and monitoring, rendering-safe, disposing, sampling, mitigating hazards and identifying weaponized and non-weaponized chemical, biological and hazardous material."

90. *Federal Bureau of Invesitgation Web Site*, 20 Feb. 2002, http://www.fbi.gov/hq/lab/org/hmru.htm, States: "The Hazardous Materials Response Unit was established in 1996 in response to the threat of terrorism involving chemical, biological, and nuclear weapons and to an expanding caseload of environmental crimes. The Unit provides the capability to safely and effectively respond to criminal acts and incidents involving the use of hazardous materials and develops the FBI's technical proficiency and readiness for crime scene and evidence-related operations in cases involving chemical, biological, and radiological materials and

wastes. This is accomplished through an integrated effort involving specialized response teams, a national training program, interagency liaison, technical assistance to FBI field and Headquarters divisions, and the development of field response programs. The Unit also trains, equips, and certifies FBI field office personnel for hazardous materials operations."

91. *The Posse Comitatus Act,* Statutes as Large 20 Sec. 145,152 (1878)

92. *Federal Bureau of Invesitgation Web Site,* 20 Feb. 2002, <http://www.fbi.gov/hq/isd/cirg/mission.htm>

93. *Federal Bureau of Invesitgation Web Site,* 20 Feb. 2002, <http://www.fbi.gov/hq/isd/cirg/tact.htm>

94. *The Goldwater-Nichols Act of 1986, Statutes at Large* 5 sec. 512(b), 1986, Senators Goldwater and Nichols sponsored legislation designed to eliminate the interservice rivalries that had effectively blocked cooperation in planning and procurement within the Pentagon.

95. Bureau of Alcohol, Tobacco and Firearms, a branch of the Treasury Department

96. General Accounting Office, *Combating Terrorism GAO/NSIAD-99-135* (Washington, D.C.: GPO, 1999)

97. The Federation of American Scientists Web Page, 12 Apr. 2002 <http://fas.org/irp/offdocs/pdd/index.html> Thirty of the sixty-three Presidential Directives (PD) that President Carter issued almost thirty years ago remain either fully or partly classified and not available for public review. Thirty-six out of seventy-five of President Clinton's National Security directives remain classified.

98. The definitions used for Governor, State and Federal Agency are verbatim from the Stafford Act (PL 93-288), all other definitions are the author's.

0-595-31628-X

www.ingramcontent.com/pod-product-compliance
Lightning Source LLC
Chambersburg PA
CBHW021239280526
45784CB00005B/2165